Odyssey of a
PHILLY BOY

Serendipity,
Tsouris
and a
Little Mazel

MEL STEIN

outskirtspress
DENVER, COLORADO

Odyssey of a Philly Boy
Serendipity, Tsouris and a Little Mazel
All Rights Reserved.
Copyright © 2013 Mel Stein
v5.0

Outskirts Press, Inc.
http://www.outskirtspress.com

ISBN: 978-1-4787-1493-4

Outskirts Press and the "OP" logo are trademarks belonging to Outskirts Press, Inc.

PRINTED IN THE UNITED STATES OF AMERICA

I dedicate this book with love to my family, each of whom has helped shape my growing up and becoming the father I never had.

To my sons, Josh and Noah:
You helped me rediscover the kid inside me and gave me the ability to become the father I aspired to be. You brought me to the realization that I was never a perfect dad and, most importantly, that I didn't have to be.

To my daughter, Alexandra:
I have had the privilege of watching you grow from a shy little girl into the confident and beautiful woman you are today. You taught me that being a daddy is different than being a dad and to always respect your character and opinions.

To my wife, Jane:
Your constant love and support have enabled me to never stop believing in myself, even during our most difficult times. Everyone needs a friend who is there not only through happy times but also through times of darkness. You are that for me.

To Shirley Stein, my mom;
Anna Lotman, my bubbe; and Morris Stein, my grandpop:
Your unconditional love is my foundation for everything.

Contents

Preface

ONE OF MY favorite quotations is from Bobby Jones, the most success-ful amateur golfer ever and a lawyer by profession. In his later years, he developed a rare spinal injury that left him bound to a wheelchair. An interviewer asked him, "Bobby, why is it you never complained once you were no longer able to play the game you loved?"

Jones' response was, "Because I play life as I have always played golf - as it lies." In my case, a series of unanticipated events forced me away from the comfortable life script I had been following. Faced with those circumstances, I started to play life by making it up as I went along, as life happened, as Bobby Jones brilliantly stated, "as it lies." This book has been thirty-six years in the making. It started when my sons, Josh and Noah, were seven and five years old, and I was thirty-two. Writing about my experiences as a single father and my feelings going through those adventures became a necessary and healthy way for me to express myself. At the time I had no idea of what use these notes would serve—maybe as a way of preserving a piece of me to share with those I love, or maybe as a primer for people in similar circumstances. Beginning this was the hardest step, but once I started, it became liberating to have the freedom to put on paper my reflections of day-to-day experiences. My original title was *The Making of a Dad—Growing Up with Josh and Noah*, but at some point I realized that this book was much more than about my being a single father. Each of us has a unique story inside, but our most meaningful ones are not about the major accomplishments of our lives. Rather, the seemingly unnoticeable events of our daily existence become the true substance of our memories. It is the richness and color of the stories about our journeys that ultimately define our character and who we truly are.

Most of what I am about to share has never been related to anyone else. In doing so I have opened up myself to you in the hope that you may gain insight into your own situations and be motivated to commit your story to writing. I have always said that what I want to be when I grow up is a writer. Now at the age of sixty-eight, I am finally entering adulthood.

Mel Stein

(I)
SETTING THE STAGE

CHAPTER 1

August 1976

Lois - gone

MY LIFE ALWAYS seemed to be on continual cruise control. From the time I was a kid, it seemed that I was always on the outside looking in. Living was a lot simpler then, never having to be involved. Now that has all changed. I am sitting on a folding chair at the beach in Fort Lauderdale's noonday sun. On a blanket next to me is Noah, who is playing in the sand with a plastic bucket and shovel. His mop of blondish hair almost covers his eyes as he diligently goes about his 'work'. It's Saturday afternoon. Josh stayed at home with Lois.

My sons are so different. Perhaps that's because Josh is older and more attuned to the reality that his parents are miserable in their marriage. Noah may be too young to understand.

I wonder if Lois intentionally wanted me to read the note she had written and left on her dresser, that she had no feelings for me, no love. We have passed the point of no return in our marriage. There is no caring between Lois and me—no touching, no communication. I now realize that the opposite of love isn't hate; it is indifference.

How much longer can I stay with her?

While I was growing up and blindly following my life script, I always thought that I was in control. There are a lot of times now that I feel so helpless, times when it's a monumental effort to get through the day.

Writing down my thoughts has become my release and my therapy.

I feel like I am in the middle of a field screaming, and no one can hear me. It hurts to think about the future.

CHAPTER 2

June 1977

IT'S NOT QUITE a year ago that I sat on this part of the beach. I was simply going through the motions of life then, doing nothing to remedy the miseries that enveloped me.

Hanging over me was the threat of a felony conviction for unknowingly possessing a stolen car I had purchased from a neighbor. My business had just gone bankrupt, and I owed eighteen thousand dollars to the Small Business Administration, which was initiating foreclosure on the second mortgage of my home. My inability to pay other debts was pushing me to declare personal bankruptcy; the IRS informed me that I owed them forty-five hundred dollars, and they wanted their money. In addition, Lois and I were facing the fact that our marriage was over.

In spite of all my self - awareness and instead of doing anything constructive, I walked around in a fog of self-pity. On top of this, even more appalling than all the problems surrounding me, was the most painful fact of all.

My hair was falling out.

Growing up, I went to Eddie the Barber at Thirtieth and Diamond Streets in North Philadelphia. After my haircuts I would go upstairs to Champ's Gym to see the boxers train. Once, after standing there in awe as I watched Sonny Liston spar, I shook hands with him. I will never forget how his huge soft paw encircled my entire hand.

Eddie the Barber would always say how wonderful and thick my hair was. He told me that I could rub manure on it, and it would still be a great head of hair.

Eddie, you promised.

Say it isn't so.

My eternal mane, preordained to outlive me, has started to suck as much as the rest of my life.

What a difference almost a year makes. Today as I sit here on the beach, I am truly at peace—enjoying the backdrop of the gentle rolling and sloshing of the ocean, listening to the almost comical yakking of some people close by, and watching a frisky dog running to catch a Frisbee.

I remember the exact moment my life changed.

I was driving my white, 1975 Cadillac Eldorado on Commercial Boulevard in Fort Lauderdale. At a traffic light, a state trooper directly behind me called out over a loudspeaker for me to pull over. Then on the side of the road, he told me to get out of the vehicle. He said that I was driving a stolen car and handcuffed me. Shaking in fear as I was riding in the back of the police car with my hands locked behind me, I had an epiphany. "What the hell am I doing?" I thought. Somehow I had the revelation that all the crap I was dealing with was not the result of "life doing it to me." I was not only responsible for all of it, but also responsible for resolving it. Sitting handcuffed in a police car was the final straw I needed to get me to realize that I own it all. This trauma was actually a well-disguised blessing, because it was at that very moment that I began to regain control of my life.

The car theft charge was dropped when I produced the bill of sale, and the police acknowledged I was totally innocent in the transaction. My business endeavors are now stabilized, and I am earning a salary that enables my sons and me to stay in our home and to set aside financial pressures, including not going forward with personal bankruptcy. I am working on an arrangement with the SBA. Even the IRS has agreed to a payment schedule of forty dollars each month. I feel like I am doing everything in my power to get my life back on track. Also I realize that I cannot achieve anything positive by worrying about it.

Lois and I are now separated but can honestly relate as friends. She decided that she needed to leave and be on her own. Living alone was her first step in becoming okay with herself. She went from a home with the "nicest person you'll ever meet" father and a domineering but well-intentioned mother, to a marriage with what she perceived as an overbearing husband. I truly understand that about her, although others may never comprehend how a mother can walk out on her children. Lois now has her own apartment and is working for a doctor. She seems to be learning how to be content with herself. Josh and Noah were well prepared for their mother's leaving, which Lois and I discussed with them prior to our separation. Of the two of us, I am definitely the more domestic one. Lois loathes housework, while I actually enjoy the mindless, immediate gratification it provides. I believe that I am the better cook and the more nurturing parent.

In some former life, I was probably a woman.

Raising my sons as a single dad in our home is the best scenario I could have ever envisioned.

CHAPTER 3

Beginning

ABOUT A YEAR before Lois left, I had an idea one day to keep a notebook and document my newly discovered awareness about the events in my life. This initial entry reflects my thoughts the first time I drove Josh to his elementary school. It was the beginning of writing about my feelings during seemingly mundane experiences. I discovered, as my marriage was winding down, that writing provided a welcome retreat that gave me comfort and satisfaction, even if I never shared what I had written with anyone.

I drove my son to school today.

A fact which might not make you sit up and take note.

It probably seems like quite an ordinary thing to do.

I bet every day millions of parents are driving their kids to school.

And I drove my son to school today.

Have you ever sat beside a very young person on a school day as he sat clutching his books and lunch box, staring out of an early morning car window, pondering all the impossible questions without answers that could fill his inquisitive mind?

"Dad, how much does the earth weigh?"

Ah yes, I drove my son to school today.

The trip is two miles and takes about four minutes.

This adds eight minutes to my twenty-three-minute drive to work since my son's school is in the opposite direction.

It was a wrinkle in my daily routine.

The frustration! Try to explain to a six-year-old, in four minutes, how anyone would actually be able to calculate the weight of the earth.

I drove my son to school today.

And when we got there, he slid over and kissed me good-bye.

He managed to gather his books and lunch box in one hand and maneuver the car door open and closed with the other.

"Bye, Dad."

I watched him from behind as he walked.

When did he get so tall?

He's a good boy. I wish I knew him better.

I love him so.

I never was a morning person,

But today I drove my son to school

And I'm really looking forward to tomorrow.

About nine years later, I was driving Josh to high school. Like every other day, I was about to hug and kiss him good-bye as I dropped him off when he proclaimed, "Dad, please don't; it's embarrassing." He had grown to my height, and I never before had considered the feelings of my now teenage son about kissing his dad in front of his school. He got out of the car, and my heart was aching.

I grew up in a home where I was never hugged or kissed by my mother and where the words "I love you" were never expressed. I agonized over Josh's request. That night, after feeling sorry for myself all day, an idea came to me that I believed would work for both of us. After dinner I sat down with Josh and proposed my resolution.

"Josh, it really means a lot to me to be able to hug and kiss you and Noah hello and good-bye and to tell you both that I love you whenever and wherever we are. I thought about this all day, and I want you to know that I respect your feelings, but please understand that I will never stop hugging and kissing you. My proposal is that I just won't do it in front of your school."

From then on we stopped two blocks away from school for our

hug and kiss, out of sight of anyone who would recognize Josh.

Noah never had a problem with my public display of affection.

To this day, no discussion, visit, letter or e-mail between Josh, Noah, and me ever ends without "I love you."

(II)
BECOMING ME

CHAPTER **4**

Poor Me

NO REALLY, I was poor. I just didn't know it at the time.

Memories of my father's gambling, his breath always reeking of alcohol, and his throwing my mother against the wall in a drunken tirade came to a welcome end when I was five years old. He left home, never to be seen again.

When I was four years old, I remember going with him on Saturdays to a dark dingy bar where he would drink beer. My meal was always a small plate of fried fish and a glass of root beer. Afterward we visited this lady and her kid. I never knew it at the time, but that was his girlfriend, and for all I knew, that could also have been his child. There was one especially memorable incident with my father that happened when I was three years old. I always thought it was a dream until years later when my mother confirmed that it actually really happened.

It was a steamy July day when my father took me to the beach in Atlantic City. He told me to stay on the blanket and watch his shoes while he went into the water. After several minutes of sitting by myself, I wandered off and eventually wound up in the water where the strong undertow pulled me under. When I flipped over and around in the waves, the salty water streamed into my nostrils and mouth. The taste of the ocean, the numbing cold, and my flailing helplessness were indelibly etched in my memory. My next recollection was being in a dim-lit room, and I was wrapped in a blanket. There were several people standing over me. My mother was crying.

I was wearing a red- and white-striped tee shirt that day. The lifeguard saw that shirt floating in the water and rescued me. If it weren't for that shirt, I wouldn't be here today.

As tough as it is after my father leaves home, we are happy and appreciate everything we have. My mom is employed as a saleslady selling dresses for Charming Shoppes in Philadelphia. Her long hours at work mean that I cannot stay at home by myself at five years of age. My sister, Marylin, then sixteen, is enrolled in a secretarial curriculum and works after school. There is no day care or preschool program, but there is a Jewish charity parochial school, Beth Jacob, which my mom discovers. The school is located on Catherine Street in South Philadelphia, about thirty minutes from our apartment. After taking me with her to work the first two weeks, my mom tells me that I am going to start school, and tomorrow a car will pick me up and take me there.

The next day, a black Buick stops in front of our apartment building. My mother walks me downstairs and outside. There is no hug or kiss good-bye when she opens the car door. I get inside, hold back the tears, and for the next half hour stare at the three other kids in the car.

No one talks.

When we finally arrive at Beth Jacob, the driver takes me to my class, which is now in its second month of the school year. All the other kids seem to understand what's happening in the classroom.

I don't have a clue.

It's kindergarten, and everyone except me knows the correct response in Hebrew to simple questions. The only Hebrew I know is my name, Mayer Hesh, which is the Hebrew version of my name, Melvin Herbert. For the first two weeks of school, my mumbling response to every question the teacher asks me is "Mayer Hesh."

She must have thought I was the village idiot.

Finally I start to get the hang of what this school is about and my knowledge and use of appropriate Hebrew increases. My teacher sees me progressing rapidly and realizes that I am a pretty smart kid.

Halfway through my kindergarten year, I get skipped into first grade, where the day is divided into English subjects in the morning and Jewish studies in the afternoon.

I become a religious fanatic at the age of five.

One day my mom brings a loaf of Italian bread home from work, and I throw it out the window, proclaiming that this is a Jewish home. This zealotry will last another year until I am old enough to attend public school.

When I come home from school there is no one there. As a result, responsibility and independence are expected from me, even at my young age. It is my job to clean the apartment, which includes emptying the ashtrays usually overflowing with my mother's cigarette butts and ashes, vacuuming the floors, and dusting. Many days I also prepare dinner, which mainly consists of making salad and lemonade, and heating the oven and inserting frozen TV dinners. Little do I know that history will repeat itself years from now when I will once again be cooking and cleaning for my family.

We live in a one-bedroom apartment in a three-story tenement at Seventh and Columbia in North Philadelphia. The bathroom is situated in a hallway that is unheated. This fact makes going to the bathroom a challenge when the temperature drops outside.

In winter the cold of the bathroom is totally overshadowed by the iciness of the bedroom, which boasts three huge bay windows that are poorly sealed. The output of heat from the steam radiator is no match for the frigid air outside. At bedtime I slip under the covers and become transfixed to one spot, unable to move, because coming in contact with the Siberian sheet in any direction would be a bone-chilling adventure. My singular goal is to warm one spot and stay there. To help me accomplish this, my mother drapes a second-hand lamb's wool coat, given to her by my aunt Gerty, on top of the blankets over me. She then lies across that pile of blankets and coat until the stinging cold has gone. As stressful as winter is, it is sharply contrasted to the brutal heat of summer.

Throughout my childhood air conditioning isn't even a thought and, in fact, we won't have anything other than an infrequent breeze coming through the screened windows until I am eleven and living in an apartment above a dress store on Lindley Avenue.

My Uncle Sam, Aunt Gerty's husband, buys a fan for us. After taking it out of the carton and reading the instructions, my mom instructs me to place it in the bedroom window. The fan has a control that allows it to blow in or out. We opt for "in" to see what it feels like. "See how nice that makes it in here," my mom proudly exclaims. "But mom, it's hot air blowing in."

After Beth Jacob, I attend two other elementary schools—Ludlow, which is about a mile's walk from our tenement, and Birney, in third grade after we move to an apartment above a butcher store at Eleventh and Louden Streets in the Logan section of North Philadelphia. It is at Birney that my "talents" start to surface and become appreciated.

I become a "safety," the kid who stands on a corner and has a white strap draped diagonally across his chest with a badge pinned on it. Standing on "my corner" in rain, snow, and heat, my job is basically to be a junior crossing guard and hold my arms out when the light is red. This keeps color-blind, mentally challenged, and little kids from crossing the street against the light. Eventually I work my way up through the ranks and become corporal of the Sixth Patrol. We are the only patrol that has its own song, which I write. We sing it every day when we march into the schoolyard after our daily street corner watch. Sung to the tune of "Turkey in the Straw," here is my first musical and literary accomplishment:

"Oh, the Sixth Patrol, the Sixth Patrol
They're always on their beat.
They're always on their corner
In rain and sleet.
Oh, they're always on their corner.
Oh, they're always on their beat.
Oh, they're always on their corner
In rain and sleet.

Have you got a poncho?
Not yet.
Are you gonna get one?
You bet!
—Sung by the Sixth Patrol Quartet

It's around this time that my mom buys me a bicycle. She tells me that she paid seven dollars for it and got it from one of her friends, who was selling her son's used bike. I am really surprised for two reasons: this is my first-ever bicycle, and by the way, I have no idea how to ride it. The two-wheeler arrives two days later. My mom is at work, and I take my "new" ride out to the cracked pavement in front of the butcher shop below our apartment. For the next several hours, I alternately get on and fall off, scraping and cutting my arms and legs on the cement. Dozens of seemingly unconcerned people pass this klutzy kid, who keeps falling off his bike. At some point, close to the three-hour mark and now bleeding from several wounds, divine intervention occurs. Miraculously, I finally 'get it' and actually remain on my bicycle. The breeze in my face feels wonderful as I cruise down the street on my new wheels.

Summertime for me is not a vacation from school but an opportunity to earn money for the family to help pay for food and clothing. I love to work and the satisfaction and sense of accomplishment that working provides. I'll never fully understand what motivates me, but I am always working, making deliveries on my bicycle for a local cleaner, doing odd jobs at my cousin's hardware store, or running errands for elderly neighbors.

Even though there are numerous times when we barely have enough food to eat—times when my mom makes her famous "potato soup," which is essentially potatoes in salted water—we survive and life is truly good.

There are countless memorable experiences of withstanding our poverty and the lessons in survival that I learn, but one of my favorite recollections occurred in the hot Philadelphia summer of 1951.

CHAPTER **5**

Origins of Character

IN 1951 TWO major newspapers, *The Inquirer*, the morning paper, and the *Philadelphia Bulletin*, the afternoon paper, were delivered to homes in and around Philadelphia. That summer the *Bulletin* truck drivers went on strike, and no *Bulletins* were delivered, even though the newspaper was still being printed. The only place anyone could purchase the newspaper was at the *Bulletin* building at Thirtieth and Market streets in Philadelphia, and there it could be bought for five cents. I saw this as an opportunity to earn extra money. Since I was left alone and in charge of the apartment during the day, I had always been trusted to do the right thing ever since I was five years old. Without someone at home to question my taking the twenty-minute ride downtown on the subway by myself, it never occurred to me that there might be dangers in having to cross a picket line of angry, hostile truck drivers. At that age I was unaware, but I would soon learn quickly, that not all people followed the Golden Rule.

On a ninety-five-degree Wednesday in July, I make my first trip to the *Bulletin* building. Walking past the strikers, I move into the massive marble building unnoticed. The truck drivers' yells and threats are focused on the adults who attempt to cross the picket line, not on a slim eight-year-old with a summer buzz cut and dressed in a white T-shirt and jeans. Once inside I am struck by the pungent, wonderful smell of fresh newsprint and the excitement of buying my first stack of newspapers. "I'll take sixty," I say to the clerk behind the counter, after calculating how many the change in my pocket will buy. I pay my three dollars and grab the neatly tied papers by the string that binds them. I know that I have to get far enough away from the *Bulletin* building to be able to sell for a dime those papers that just cost me a nickel.

On my way out, a few strikers notice me with my papers and scream insults my way. "Just keep moving," I tell myself. Staring at the ground in front of me, my head down and resolute, I walk ten blocks to Twentieth and Market and set up shop on the corner. Many of the hundreds of people who walk by happily purchase their favorite newspaper from me, even at twice the price. A few people who are strikers, their friends, or family members spit and curse at me as they walk by. One even throws an empty cigarette pack at me, but I try not to think about the potential danger from those few angry people. To stay focused on what I have to do, I sing to myself. I love music, and I know all the words of every popular tune. Singing is a diversion I can always count on to help me take my mind off any fear I might have. Within an hour I have sold out of papers and feel very proud of myself. In fact, I am so pleased with what I have just accomplished that I beam as I get back on the subway, and I keep smiling all the way home.

Thursday is just like Wednesday. I buy sixty papers, sell them and, after a job well done, go home in an hour. On Friday there seems to be a lot more people in town, and I am able to sell my papers in half my now usual time. I go back to the *Bulletin* building and buy and then sell a second stack. At this point my profit for the three days is eleven dollars, less the subway fares and one five-cent Hershey bar I treat myself to each day. Amazingly I keep this job a secret from my mom.

On Saturday and Sunday, I stay home with my mother who is off from work and who certainly wouldn't approve of my going downtown alone and selling newspapers in the middle of a strike. When Monday comes, I am back in business, going to the *Bulletin* building and again selling my sixty papers in about an hour. The next day, Tuesday, however, would prove to be a defining moment in my life. It would test my courage, it would test my strength, and it would reveal my character.

The strike, now in its second week, continues with no end in sight. I take my regular subway trip downtown to the *Bulletin*. I cross the picket line and experience the curses and threats I have learned to drown out by singing to myself Rosemary Clooney's "Come On-a My House" or Teresa Brewer's "Music, Music, Music." Stepping up to the window to purchase my usual stack of sixty newspapers, I place my three dollars on the well-worn wooden counter. What I see next shocks me. At first I think a mistake had been made.

"I only want sixty," I state.

"That's what's there, kid," the clerk replies.

Somehow my normal manageable bundle of papers has grown to two and a half times its normal size, nearly one-third of my height!

The clerk adds, "Tuesday's paper is full of ads!"

Wednesday night all the stores stay open late in center city Philadelphia, and the Tuesday *Bulletin* contains extra advertising sections to attract Wednesday night shoppers. Being very slight for my age, I can barely lift the stack of papers off the counter. I manage to drag them outside where the noonday heat is approaching one hundred degrees. Both my heart and head ache as I realize that I can never make it all the way to Twentieth and Market with those newspapers. I pull and drag the bundle of sixty papers along the ground as far as I am able, which is eight blocks away to Twenty-second and Market. The string has cut into my fingers, and I wipe my hand on my starched jeans, leaving a red stain on the side. Sweat streams down my forehead, and I can't tell whether it is my sweat or my tears that leave its mark on the sleeve of my T-shirt that I use to wipe my face. Somehow I manage to gather enough courage, sing a verse of Nat King Cole's "Too Young," and look at the task at hand. Although the bottom paper is ruined from scraping along the ground, I still have fifty-nine papers that I can sell. The heat is stiflingly unbearable, and my arms ache from the strain of dragging that bundle for eight blocks. It takes every ounce of strength and determination I possess to make it as far as I've gone. After an hour in the broiling heat, I still have twenty unsold papers.

My head is now pounding, and waves of nausea make me feel like I could puke at any moment. One passerby, a strike sympathizer, flicks cigarette ashes in my face, but I won't go home until I sell the final twenty papers. I have to get to a cooler place, and it occurs to me that the subway train will not only provide relief from the heat but also a new audience of customers. In the next twenty minutes on the train home, I walk from car to car until finally, just one stop before I reach home, I sell the last paper.

There were no high fives in 1951, and most people were not in touch with their inner selves, but I still remember how proud I felt after I sold that last newspaper. "You did it; you did it!" I kept repeating to myself. I never told my mother about the newspapers because I didn't want to upset her or have her worry about me.

I have recounted this story to my sons and daughter in hopes that they might learn that we all have a choice in life, as I discovered on that steamy Tuesday in 1951. Either we become victims of our troubles and experience our lives feeling sorry for ourselves, or we use those hard times as springboards by realizing that we all have the capacity to make it through any adversity. Knowing that we have that choice is very powerful.

Most people believe that a turning point in life comes as a result of some major, earth-shattering event.

In reality, pivotal moments in our lives come from seemingly insignificant experiences that might often go unnoticed and forgotten—incidents that truly help define who we are.

CHAPTER **6**

Key Life Lessons

WE ALL KNOW people whose contribution to our lives is rarely appreciated and probably never acknowledged.

My second cousin, Bert, was at least forty years my senior and someone who I can truly say had a profound effect on my life. Although I can recount only two memorable discussions I had with him, they were lessons that would positively impact my character and remain with me today. With basically no male figure in my life that I could emulate as I was growing up, I was fortunate to have someone like Bert to help guide me. One such experience happened when I was eight years old.

It was the first time we met, and I shook hands with him. He looked me straight in the eye and said, "Shake hands like you mean it!"

He squeezed my hand tightly to demonstrate.

To this day I remember that experience and regard a firm handshake as the initial expression of solid character.

My other memorable experience with Cousin Bert occurred a few years later.

I want a job over Christmas vacation, and my mother suggests that I call my cousin, whose busiest weeks for his bakery supply company happen around the holidays. Although I am mature and self-sufficient beyond my years, I am still a loner and a shy kid who isn't used to asking others for assistance. My phone call with Bert this day is something I will always remember.

I start out by saying, "My mother told me to call and ask you for a job over the Christmas break."

He replies, "Does your mother want a job or do you"?

His comment hits me like a lightning bolt, and I immediately understand.

This simple exchange will forever change my ability to take initiative and to be assertive. Over the two-week vacation, I work at Bert's company packing boxes for shipment and helping with the mailing of his holiday greetings.

In those two weeks, I learned to take orders, to have a production responsibility, to solve problems on the fly, and to take complete ownership of my job.

In those two weeks I discovered a lot about being an adult.

CHAPTER 7

My Mom

IN MY ENTIRE childhood, I never remember my mom kissing me, hugging me, or telling me she loved me, but I always knew that I was loved. All of my clothes were hand-me-downs from an older cousin, but they were always clean and pressed. As a fourth grader I actually won the "Best-Dressed Boy" award and received a used copy of Mark Twain's *Pudd'nhead Wilson* as a prize. Other than schoolbooks, this was the first book that I actually owned. I believe that my love of books started the day I received that book. From the wonderful smell of the pages to the pride I felt holding and reading it, *Pudd'nhead Wilson* provided me with a sense of comfort and satisfaction that I had never previously experienced. Starting with that single volume, the library in my office today is packed from floor to ceiling with books that I have acquired and read along my life's path.

From the age of six until I am twelve, each summer my mom and I take the Greyhound bus to Atlantic City for a week's vacation. Along with the neatly packed suitcase, we each carry a paper bag containing lunch, which my mom prepared before we left. We happily consume the sandwich and soda during the two-hour bus trip. Once we get there, we stay at a boarding house, go to the beach every day, and to the movies or Steel Pier at night. A long walk on the boardwalk and a stop at Kohr's Frozen Custard is always part of the evening, before the jitney ride back to where we are staying. Although it is never discussed, as a kid I am aware that my mom sacrifices to give me that annual trip. I don't know how or where it comes from, but even at that age I never take anything for granted.

Late in life she was consumed with dementia. As a result of her mental state, she started confusing me with my drunk and abusive father.

I cried after every visit to the nursing home.

A few days before she passed away, I sat next to her, holding her hand as she slept soundly. It had been several months since she last recognized me, and just as I was about to leave, she opened her eyes.

"Mel," she said as she looked at me in her last lucid moment.

Her eyes closed a few seconds later, never to open again.

My mother was the youngest of eight children. When Anna and Morris Lotman came to the United States from Russia in 1904, they arrived with all the hopes and dreams that come with building a new life in a new country. Both had remarried after losing their first spouses to illness in the harsh climate of the Russian winters. Morris knew that Anna had three children from her previous marriage: Ida, the eldest; Rifka; and Rae, the youngest. But when the guests had all departed the wedding hall, a baby remained in the corner. "Whose baby is that?" questioned Morris to his new bride. "I was afraid to tell you," replied Anna, "but she's mine also." The kindhearted Morris, a bit shocked, accepted the response, laughed, and welcomed baby Esther into the new family along with her three siblings. That's how it was in the "old country"—arranged marriages, a sense of family that enveloped everyone, and an eternal hope that life would always be good.

And so their life began in a home above a store in the Frankford section of Philadelphia. The trolley tracks outside transported the citizens of the city past the general store that would provide the economic foundation for the Lotman family.

Morris had been a merchant in Russia and invests all of his savings that he brings with him to start Lotman's General Store. Anna purchases the clothing while Morris focuses on the glassware, pots, and pans with which he is familiar. Everyone works, including the baby as soon as she can walk. The business grows and prospers, as does the Lotman family.

Together, Morris and Anna have four children: Samuel, Reba, Albert, and finally, Sara, who will eventually become my mother. Sara is born in 1910, around the time of an influenza epidemic. Without antibiotics the sickly Esther dies of pneumonia at the age of seven.

Morris and Anna become Zeda and Bubbe to all who know them.

From the few pictures that remain, Morris, with his long white hair and flowing beard, exemplifies the pride, determination, and work ethic that are expected of any immigrant in the early 1900s. His title, Zeda, reflects the respect that not only his children but also his customers have for this deeply religious and caring man. Make no mistake about it though, Zeda is in charge, and he demands adherence to the rules of the house. The only one who is given special dispensation is his youngest, Sara, or Shirley as they call her.

Anna, a large woman who speaks with a heavy Yiddish accent is everyone's Bubbe. She is Bubbe personified, and she exudes love. The one picture of her that is displayed in numerous descendants' homes today has her seated in an armchair by a fireplace. Her girth fills out the entire chair, but she is still beautiful. The smile on her face could pass for the Mona Lisa—enigmatic but warm and embracing. Years later, after Zeda passed away, Bubbe lives with my mother, my sister and me. I remember explicitly how wonderful our home always smells, overflowing with the delectable aroma of Bubbe's cooking. I love her so much that at the age of three, I speak with her Yiddish accent. No one would ever expect to hear "Vait a minute I go mit choo" coming out of the mouth of a three-year old.

Bubbe and Zeda are the unifying link for all of their children. They are the strength, the glue, and the foundation that provide absolute respect for family. Life in Frankford becomes extremely rewarding. With the collective hard work of all the Lotmans comes great wealth. The only one who is absolved from the rigor of the retail store is Shirley, Zeda's favorite. As a young lady, she is chauffeured, but ironically she will be the only woman in the family who will have to work all of her adult life. For the six remaining children, each develops his or her family. Although none goes to college, all except Shirley become financially secure and have relatively happy lives in marriage.

Shirley smokes at an early age and eventually becomes a chain-smoker, three packs a day until the age of seventy. Amazingly, one day she quits cold turkey, never to light up again. After that she tells me that she frequently has dreams about smoking but has the strength to resist the temptation.

As a child Shirley disregards curfews imposed by Zeda, and she sneaks into the house late at night. Even when he catches her, Zeda's only punishment for his little girl is a reprimand.

At the age of twenty-four, Shirley marries my father, Lou—handsome, brilliant, and cavalier. Lou has a voracious appetite for knowledge. Although he never finishes high school, he is always reading. The only positive memory about her husband that my mother would relate is that when he runs out of books or magazines to read, he studies the encyclopedia. As a result, he develops a vast knowledge about a lot of things. Unfortunately, Lou believes that hard work is beneath him. When he is given numerous opportunities to prove himself with his brothers-in-law, Al and Sam, he fails miserably. He eventually turns to alcohol as a refuge. After six years of unhappy marriage, Lou leaves Shirley, only to return four years later for a second chance. It is then that they have me.

An interesting observation is that everyone in my family refers to me as Melvin, and so do I when I speak to members of my family.

To the rest of the world, I am Mel.

It's 1948, and I am five years old. My father leaves my mother again, this time for good. Lou looks like Clark Gable and goes to Hollywood to become a movie star. Alcohol eventually leads to Lou's demise.

One day, when I am twenty-four, I am beginning my third year of pharmacy school. My wife, Lois, has just stopped working and is pregnant with our first son, Josh. I have no money to pay the tuition for school. Dropping out is becoming my only recourse, because I need fifteen hundred dollars, and I have no other options.

It has now been almost twenty years since I have heard from my father, but this week I receive a letter that turns out to be one of several miracles with which I have been blessed.

The letter is from a friend of Louis Stein who states that my father wanted to contact me over the years, but could never bring himself to do so, mostly because of the shame he felt from abandoning his family years before. He goes on to state that my father wanted me to have the enclosed check as his legacy to me.

This has to be an act of God, because the amount of the check is, unbelievably, exactly fifteen hundred dollars.

Louis Stein dies a ward of the State of California and is buried there in a public cemetery.

My mother is not book-smart, but she is definitely a woman ahead of her time as a single, working mom. She accepts her lot in life with no complaints and is never envious of others, but instead she is happy for them and their successes. In a time when crossing racial and ethnic barriers isn't popular, she has friends of all colors and religions who visit our humble home. As a salesperson, her customers and peers love her for her friendship and caring. She is never too tired or self-absorbed to help others.

I remember a young couple, George and Ellen Boychevsky, who recently emigrated from Poland and were living in our tenement. They spoke broken English, and my mom befriended them. They told my mother that they were brokenhearted, because they had to leave their dog, Muzik, behind in Poland. My mother called the immigration service, obtained the necessary paperwork, and three months later, Muzik was reunited with his tearful owners.

As she got older, my mom's life of toil took its toll on her health—severe debilitating arthritis, congestive heart failure, and eventually senile dementia. It saddens me that most of the memories that Josh, Noah, and Alexandra have of their grandmother are those of a crotchety old woman.

For me she is a model of commitment, selflessness, sacrifice, caring, and integrity.

CHAPTER **8**

Morris Stein

THERE WERE THREE people in my childhood who I can truly say loved me unconditionally: my mom, Bubbe, and Grandpop, my father's father.

Morris Stein made his living as a tailor. Prior to immigrating to America through Ellis Island in the early 1900s, he was a cavalryman in the Austrian army. He married the love of his life, Mary, who was twenty years younger, and together they had two children, Louis, my father, and Claire. After ten years of marriage, Mary broke Morris's heart by leaving him for a younger man. For this most gentle and loving man, the grief and loneliness he endured must have been unbearable. During all the time I knew him, Grandpop never raised his voice or spoke a harsh word about anyone

Mary died from influenza soon after she left, sometime around 1918. It was then that Morris became a single parent.

After his children were grown and gone, Morris lived alone in Camden, New Jersey. Once my father left our home, Grandpop would come and visit my mother, my sister, and me in our apartment every Sunday. I don't know how many modes of public transportation he had to take to get from Camden to North Philadelphia, but whatever the time of year and regardless of the weather, he showed up each Sunday morning. On every visit he was dressed in a three-piece suit and a tie. His greetings when he walked in the door were always the same. "Hello to Shirley, hello to mine sveetheart (my sister Marylin), and hello to mine sveetheart's brother—Melly, Melly, Melly." Marylin was GrandPop's 'sveetheart', because she was named for his wife, Mary.

Grandpop would then take from his pocket and hand me a little bag containing all the goodies people would leave in their clothes that he was tailoring in the past week. I loved the surprise and the collection of pens, rabbit's feet, and assorted pocket fillers that were in the bag each week. I still have a silver-looking piece that is the shape of a horseshoe. In its center is a penny, and the inscription around the penny reads, "Keep Me and Never Go Broke." When I am five years old, Grandpop teaches me how to play pinochle, and every Sunday we sit and play all afternoon until he goes home.

There are two distinct similarities between my grandfather and me. In addition to our both being single parents, Morris's children, Louis and Claire, would spend all of their adult lives not speaking to each other. I could never understand how a brother and sister could treat each other like that.

In my early life, my sister who is ten years my senior, was like a second mother. Without a television, my sister would read to me, or we would enjoy listening to radio programs together. The adventures of *Buck Rodgers of the 21st Century*, *Mr. Keane, Tracer of Lost Persons* and *The Shadow* provided fantasies to transport us, even momentarily, out of our humble surroundings. When I was seven years old I demonstrated my love for her by taking all the money I had at that time, $6.91, and went by myself to buy a rhinestone bracelet for her birthday. That bracelet shined like nothing I had ever seen. The saleslady said that I needed fourteen cents more. I went back home and looked for change that dropped behind the sofa cushions. It took that and going through the neighbor's trash to find a few empty soda bottles that I returned for the deposit to get the additional change I needed. It was the most beautiful gift I could imagine, and I remember how proud I was to give it to her.

I can honestly tell you that as much as I loved my sister when I was a kid, I really have no idea how and why the relationship between Marylin and me turned disastrous and became similar to that of Louis and Claire's.

The separation of a family develops in a slow, insidious process, somewhat like a cancer. We all go about our daily lives while minor, unresolved exchanges occur until one day they reach clinical proportions, and we finally take notice. Brothers, sisters and cousins have children and grandchildren. People die, and others move away. Someone does not talk to someone else for a meaningless reason. Factions develop and sides are taken. Jealousy and envy create further chasms.

And then it all becomes apparent like the climax of a Peter Sellers *Pink Panther* movie. Everyone in the film brings her or his own slice of drama to a tumultuous finale. In the movies, it's a race with an ultimate convergence of all characters. Crashes and hysteria abound. Finally, the dust settles, sensibility rules, and happiness and resolution occur.

But that is in the movies. In real life the outcome is not so dramatic or wonderful.

To this day my wife and I have no idea why my sister is so angry. In addition to her verbal and written abuse toward us, Marylin never speaks to our daughter, Alexandra, or even acknowledges her existence.

Why? It is a question without an answer.

What is clear to me is that relationships, especially in families, are very complex and fragile. They require constant nurturing and can never be assumed or taken for granted.

I have been blessed to have a mother, a bubbe and a grandpop who gave me unconditional love as I was growing up.

Grandpop stopped visiting when I was nine years old. He developed atherosclerosis and ultimately senile dementia and went to live in the Workmen's Circle home in Media, Pennsylvania. Once a month we visited him until I was twelve years old. It was then that he passed away. We buried him in a cemetery in New Jersey, near

Camden, where he lived most of his life.

Morris Stein was love and kindness personified. I am honored to carry on his legacy.

At the same time, I am disappointed in myself that my level of intolerance as I have gotten older is a contradiction to whom he was.

(III)
DRUGS AND ROCK AND ROLL

CHAPTER 9

My First Fortuitous Event

IT'S 1957 AND a few months after I turn fourteen, my mom and I move in with my sister and brother-in-law in Plymouth Meeting, Pennsylvania. They have just bought their first house, and my mother is paying them rent so they can afford their mortgage. At the time I am attending the smart boys' school in Philadelphia: Central High, class number 215. Every class at Central has a number, which creates bonds of friendship for life. One of my fondest memories at Central is my first experience in the marching band when I was fourteen and in ninth grade.

As I look back on my life, most signposts point toward my drums being at the center of almost every major turning point. Playing the drums would be the reason I received my first scholarship. They enabled me to pay for eight years of college. My drums were the link that directed me to go to pharmacy school and eventually would lead me to my life's career as a healthcare executive. They helped rescue my home from foreclosure in Florida. The details of these events will be explained in later chapters, but the fact is that even though she couldn't afford it, my mom bought me my first drum set when I was eleven years old. She bought those Slingerland drums on the installment plan from Wurlitzer's at Eighth and Walnut in Philadelphia. Every Saturday when I went downtown on the subway for my music lesson, I would tear the next page in the installment book and make the weekly payment with the dollars my mom had given me.

Mastering a musical instrument comes naturally to some people, but that wasn't the case for me. My fervor to be a drummer drove me to practice, but learning to play was literally about creating new pathways in my brain to be able to play four separate beats at the same time with my hands and feet. The ability to gain independence for my four extremities did not come easily. It took weekly drum lessons, endless practicing, and playing along with records at home for the last three years, to get me to a point where I was ready to perform.

So here I am, a member of the marching band at Central High School. The only problem is that, as the newest member of the drum line, the instrument I am directed to play is not the snare drum.

It is the cymbals.

This is our first practice in early September, and the weather outside is rainy and cold. Instead of field practice, the fifty-plus member marching band is rehearsing in the band room where the acoustics are less than desirable. The piece is a famous march that begins with the trumpets blaring, Ta ta ta ta, ta ta, ta ta, ta da, and then a bass drum boom, followed by a cymbal crash (me).

It takes the trumpets almost thirty minutes to get their opening "ta tas" correct. It's really, really loud in the room, and those of us in the drum line amuse ourselves by telling jokes while the trumpets agonizingly rehearse their part. Finally it's time to move on, and I am more than ready for my inaugural performance. At that moment the comedian in me seizes the opportunity and puts down the cymbals and picks up a metal triangle I spot in a nearby box.

And so it follows that the bandmaster counts down, the trumpets commence their ta ta ta ta, ta ta, ta ta, ta da, and the bass drum booms; but instead of the anticipated cymbal crash, I strike the triangle—ting.

The band members think it's really funny, so amusing that some are brought to tears. The bandmaster does not. He scowls at me, screams "Stein," and throws me out of the marching band for the next two weeks.

For the past year and a half, I had walked about two miles to Central from our apartment in Philadelphia. Now that I live in Plymouth Meeting, it takes me over an hour and two bus rides to commute, but since Central High is the best public school in the Philadelphia area, I think nothing of my daily trip.

It is now the second half of my sophomore year, and a month ago I developed strep throat and was sick at home for five days. The privilege of attending Central at no cost is given only to residents of Philadelphia. After moving to the suburbs, I changed my information form at school from our apartment to my aunt Reba's address in Philadelphia and listed her phone number as my contact number.

This was my first-ever prolonged illness, and I was unaware that after a three-day absence the school calls home. When the school called my aunt's number, Uncle Bill, clueless to my ruse, answered the phone. His direct and honest response was, "He doesn't live here." My secret was out, and I only learned of this when I returned to school the following week and was called to the principal's office. He politely explained that I could still attend Central, but the cost would be eighteen hundred dollars a year. He might as well have said eighteen million. My heart weighed heavy. My only option was to drop out of Central and attend the school closest to my new home. That school was Plymouth-Whitemarsh (PW) High School.

Although I am distressed beyond belief to leave Central and my friends, this change of scholastic venue turns out to be an especially fortuitous moment in my life.

At Central everyone was smart, and I was an average fish in a huge pond. At PW, I place in the advanced class, make the JV baseball team, and join the marching band, dance band, and a rock band: the HiFi's.

And best of all, at PW there are girls!

Across the street from my house in Plymouth Meeting lives Philip Nemchek and his family. Philip's father, Maxwell, is the manager of Green Valley Country Club, located in nearby Lafayette Hill. Maxwell Nemchek is only about five feet tall, but from the parking lot, you can hear him screaming in the kitchen "You can kiss my royal Canadian ass if you don't hurry up with these orders." He is a pit bull on the outside and a puppy once you get to know him. I tell Philip that I would love to work as a busboy at Green Valley, and he takes me over to meet his dad. Maxwell hires me on the spot, and during the next few months, I earn Maxwell's respect as a result of my hard work. He promotes me to head busboy. I also become the chef in the men's grill on weekends.

Every Saturday and Sunday morning, I get picked up at my house at 5:30 a.m. by one of the kitchen guys who drives the Green Valley station wagon. When I arrive at work, my initial tasks include squeezing a case of oranges for fresh juice, slicing a dozen tomatoes and onions (I always use a separate knife for the onions), and cutting strips of lox and sturgeon for the early breakfast diners.

I then get on a stepstool, so I can reach into the tops of the huge coffee urns and scrub the insides to remove the bitter residue. Everyone always said that I made the best coffee, because evidently I was the only one who cleaned those urns. After running water through, I freshly brew the regular and decaf.

The huge walk-in meat refrigerator is upstairs from the grillroom in the back of the kitchen. That is where the corned beef and beef tongue are kept floating in vats of cold, briny water. After fishing with my hand in those icy tanks for the cold cuts du jour, I take my prizes downstairs to the grillroom kitchen where I slice a few pounds of each for the lunch orders. Once all of my setups are complete, I have about twenty minutes left before the 7:00 a.m. early birds arrive. This time is spent making myself a nice lox, tomato, and onion sandwich on a fresh bagel. At my first chance to sit down, I peacefully savor my breakfast and wash it down with a large glass of that sweet orange juice before the breakfast orders start streaming in from the waitresses in the grillroom.

Later in the day, from the side window that opens to the swimming pool, I fill orders for the thickest milkshakes ever created along with various frozen fruit concoctions I dream up, which all contain lime ice as the base. My work behind that counter is nothing short of joyous. The members like me, and I will eventually date several of their cute daughters.

As the chef in the grill, I befriend the head golf pro, George Griffin Jr., by making him super-huge sandwiches for lunch. He repays the favor by giving me golf lessons on Mondays when the club is open for the help but closed to the members. George also gives me an ancient set of clubs to use. I become a fair golfer, playing every Monday and carrying my clubs around the course along with some of the kitchen help who also are "golfers." This goes on for the two years I work there.

After golf, we play poker.

One Monday Jimmy Price, a buddy of mine from the kitchen, prepares a large quantity of freshly squeezed orange juice and an equal amount of vodka that the six of us playing cards imbibe in the two hours of poker.

This is the first time I am ever drunk, and my only thought when Jimmy is driving me home is that dying probably would be preferable to how I am feeling. Upon arriving at my house, I tumble out of the car door and crawl up the lawn, puking my guts out. Once inside I speak to no one, and I wind up sleeping the next twenty-four hours.

My mom thinks I have a stomach virus.

Soon thereafter I will give up golf until many years later, when I join Meadowlands Country Club in nearby Blue Bell. (See Chapter 53.)

Along the way at Green Valley, I become pals with all of the bands that play at the frequent Saturday night dinner dances. My friendship with the bandleaders is rewarded one week when one of them, Marty Portnoy, asks me if I would like to sit in on the drums for the next set. "Are you kidding?" I reply and happily switch my busboy jacket for the drummer's too large tux jacket. Needless to say I am in my glory playing the drums with Marty's band. After the set I put back on my busboy attire and return to my duties when the then-president of Green Valley, Harry Sall, calls me over and expresses his delight in hearing me play. He asks about my plans for school, and I tell him that I am beginning Temple University in the fall. I explain, "My high school grades are excellent as are my SAT scores, but my college choices and applications were limited to two, based solely on the distance to commute. I was accepted to both Temple University and the University of Pennsylvania but chose Temple because the cost was so much less than Penn's Ivy League tuition."

Mr. Sall listens to my story and asks me, "Would you like a scholarship for your first year at Temple?"

"Oh my God, yes," I almost scream out.

He tells me that the scholarship will be from the Golden Slipper Square Club. Even though I chose Temple based on my financial ability, without this stipend I still don't have sufficient savings to cover my cost. The scholarship is an absolute blessing.

CHAPTER **10**

How I Started My Music Career

FOR AS LONG as I can remember, I wanted to be a doctor when I grew up. It was my belief that a prerequisite to that goal was majoring in biology in college. This preconception was never discussed with anyone, nor did I have any realization that kids got into medical school by majoring in all kinds of other subjects. In spite of finding most of my biology courses fascinating, especially histology, cell physiology, mammalian anatomy, and genetics, my grades were not sufficient to give me even a sniff of medical school.

Although I was a smart kid and an excellent student throughout grade school, it came way too easy for me. With no one at home to guide or assist me, I never learned how to study or how to be disciplined and organized with my schoolwork. Based on my total lack of preparation, college was a rude awakening.

It's September 1961, and I am starting my adventure in higher education at Temple University. The bright sunshine and brisk fall air are a great backdrop to the multitude of freshmen rushing around and getting acclimated to their college surroundings on North Broad Street in Philadelphia. In the midst of finding my way around the campus and my vain attempt to get organized in my studies, I decide to pledge a fraternity. This is absolute insanity on my part, especially since at this moment I am confusing my math class with a foreign language. Even more obvious is the fact that I have just enough money, with my scholarship, for tuition, books, and all other college essentials.

I certainly have no additional funds to join a fraternity.

The frat I pledge is Tau Epsilon Phi (TEP). During the process, while some of my pledge brothers are subjected to treatment that at times borders on inhumane, the worst that I have to endure is reciting the Greek alphabet backward three times while holding a lighted match. I become quite proficient at this.

In fact, if I did as well in my studies as I did in learning to rapidly recite the Greek alphabet backward, today I would be a brain surgeon or possibly leader of the free world.

On "hell night" our pledge class is kept in a dark room, and we are summoned one by one to whatever unknown "punishment" awaits us. It is terrifying, especially the screaming that those of us remaining in the darkness can hear from outside the door. When it's finally my turn, I am escorted out of the room and down a flight of stairs to the outside. The pledge master looks at me and tells me to "Go home." Overcome with joy and relief, I am out of there as quickly as my legs can carry me. "I was never a wise ass, and I guess they like me" is my rationale while I ruminate on what just happened as I make my way home.

One of the TEP brothers, Steve, is the social director. One day I hear him discussing plans for an upcoming party and that he is looking for a band.

"I have a band, and we're available that night," I tell him.

Amazingly, sight unseen, Steve and I negotiate a price, and I am hired. The only problem for me is that I actually neither have a band nor am I a member of someone else's.

The reality is that on two occasions, at other fraternity parties, I have heard a group that I really like. Later that day I approach the bandleader of that group, Ben Geaver, and mention that I have a gig for him. I emphasize the singular stipulation: I am to be the drummer.

And so in 1961 my professional music career is launched.

A few months later, I book a band job at the Warwick Hotel in center city Philadelphia. The hotel is all union, and as a result any musician playing there must be a member of the musicians' union. Between classes I take the subway downtown to the Union Hall on North Eighteenth Street. With my drumsticks in hand, I go to the office of the guy who tests you to make sure that you have the musical proficiency to be a member of Local 77. The problem I encounter is that "the guy" is out to lunch, and I can't wait for him to return because I have a class in an hour. The only person I can find there at this time is the treasurer of the union. I tell him of my predicament— that the testing guy is gone, and I have a gig this coming Saturday night and need to be in the union in order to play at the Warwick. He looks at me and asks, "Do you have the money to pay your union fees today?" I eagerly reply, "Yes."

"OK, you're in" is his response.

As an aside, although I enjoyed the pledge process at TEP that included going on a pledge trip to Rensselaer Polytechnic Institute in Troy, New York, when the night comes to be inducted into the fraternity, I choose not to join.

I simply can't afford it.

CHAPTER 11

The VIPs

FROM THAT FIRST fraternity party gig at TEP, I start playing once or twice every weekend with Ben Geaver and also a few other bands. While playing at various parties and college mixers, I meet a lot of musicians. One day, in the middle of my sophomore year, I receive a call from Joel Shane, the trumpet and bass player for The VIPs, a rock band. All of the guys in the group are Temple students.

Joel heard me play at a dance in Mitten Hall and says that his group is looking for a new drummer. I jump at the chance and agree to play with them the following weekend. After passing the "test," I become an official VIP.

The configuration of the group on stage has me sitting in the center at my drums. Joel (trumpet and bass) and Steve (guitar) are on my left in front of me and Joey (keyboard) and Gerry (tenor and alto sax) on the right. Joey plays a Hammond organ, and the huge Leslie speakers are set up behind me as are all the other speakers for the instruments and microphones.

My ears ring for two weeks after that first night, and from that day forward I will forever have a hearing loss in the upper range. We are loud, but each of us is a better than average musician. Everyone except me sings very well. Our music consists of the whole James Brown show, The Beatles and other English groups, The Righteous Brothers, Soul Survivors, Motown, and popular songs like "Runaround Sue" and "Sherry."

Along the way we are privileged to work with Bobby Rydell, Chubby Checker, and Lee Andrews and the Hearts, and to record for Swan Records in South Philadelphia. As a bit of background, The Beatles' smash record of "She Loves You" and Freddy "Boom Boom" Cannon's hit "Palisades Park" were both released on Swan Records. The Swan label was distributed by Cameo-Parkway Records, which was formed in 1956 by Cal Mann and Bernie Lowe. Cal Mann co wrote with Bernie Lowe and Dave Appell a number of major rock-and-roll hits, including Elvis Presley's "Teddy Bear," Bobby Rydell's "Wild One," and Chubby Checker's "Let's Twist Again" and "Limbo Rock." Cal Mann and Dave Appell discovered The VIPs at a rock concert we were playing. They co wrote the song "Would You Believe," which we recorded at Swan's studios and on the Swan label. The backup singers on our record were two very talented young ladies known as Dawn, as in Tony Orlando and Dawn.

With our four-part harmonies; strong, tight playing; remarkable good fortune; and connections; The VIPs were destined to become rock stars.

There is just one problem: a singular glitch that had been baked into our DNA.

All of us, except Joey, were schmucks when it came to realizing that perhaps we were really meant to be career musicians. Joey was the only VIP whose goal it was to be a musician after college. Gerry, tenor and alto sax (sometimes he plays both at the same time with different fingering!), was going to law school. Joel wanted to be an English teacher and Steve, a psychologist.

Each of us loves what we do together every time we step on stage but never thinks for one moment that maybe we should do this as our vocation. Instead we are all blindly following our "preordained" life script.

Two important facts about The VIPs:

Our secret is that we are the only ones who know what "VIPs" actually stands for: Very Important Psychotic Screamers.

Although there are five of us and each has a microphone, my microphone isn't connected to anything. In spite of that, I still sing along with every tune. With that said, there are two songs, "King of the Road" and "Mrs. Brown, You Got a Lovely Daughter," that I get up from my drummer's throne, come to the front of the stage, and stand in the spotlight and sing with backup harmonies by my four friends.

This is the era of The Beatles and all of The VIPs have long hair. One of the greatest highlights of my music career is the legion of screaming girls when I sing those two songs.

As extraordinary as our experiences together were, after five years of playing and working together—brothers under the skin—we all eventually go our separate ways and sadly have not reconnected since.

The same lack of thought about a possible future as a career VIP goes into my decision to go to pharmacy school and to marry Lois.

CHAPTER **12**

Pharmacy School

ONE OF THE musicians I meet before joining The VIPs is an up-right bass player named Joe Mogilefsky. He's in his third year at Temple's School of Pharmacy and works in his dad's store, Mogilefsky Pharmacy, at Seventh and Columbia in North Philadelphia. Joe and I become good friends. One day when it becomes clear to me as a Temple undergrad that my grades aren't going to get me into medical school, I have a discussion with Joe regarding what I am going to do next with my life. "Why don't you go to pharmacy school, get your grades up, and then get into medical school?" Joe suggests.

"Hey, that sounds like a good idea" is my immediate response. Without giving it a second thought, I literally walk into Temple University School of Pharmacy on North Broad Street in June 1965 and meet with Fred Gable, assistant dean. He accepts me into the pharmacy program while I am standing there. At this time all that is required to go to pharmacy school is one year of liberal arts, and I have a four-year BA degree. Mr. Gable suggests that I go to pharmacy school this summer; then I will have only two more years, instead of four, to complete my pharmacy degree. But it is never my goal to finish pharmacy school and become a pharmacist. My belief is that I will get exemplary grades in pharmacy school, and in a year or so, those better grades will enable me to be accepted to medical school.

Even more importantly, this summer The VIPs are booked to play in Wildwood, New Jersey, at the Manor Hotel with the Minsky's Follies.

We are playing in the lounge, and The Follies are in the grand ballroom. To get to the stage in the lounge, we have to walk through the dressing room where the showgirls are in various stages of getting into their outfits. On our first sortie through that dressing room, the five twenty-year-old VIPs almost have a collective heart attack, trying not to stare at the spectacular, unclad female bodies all around us. Some of the girls giggle at our demeanor but do nothing to cover up their nakedness.

I once had a lab instructor in organic chemistry who described all men as "leering, prancing goats." At that moment that is exactly what we are.

After a week of this stumbling stroll, we become desensitized to this wonderful sight. The VIPs and the Minsky's Follies showgirls are one big happy family. We actually have conversations with the girls as the five of us take our time and very slowly wend our way through the dressing room to our stage in the lounge.

Four of The VIPs rent an apartment for the summer. Steve, our guitar player, stays at his parents' place. The front door of our apartment opens into a kitchen/living room with a bathroom on the side. At the back, on either side, is a bedroom. Joey and I take the bedroom on the right, and Joel and Gerry share the one on the left.

This is now June, and a few months before, during spring break, we played at Tony Mart's, a huge nightclub located in Summers Point, New Jersey. Across from Tony Mart's is a restaurant known for its roast beef sandwiches, The Coach's Corner, owned by a guy who had coached college football. The sign proudly displayed on the outside wall of his restaurant announces "Beef and Conversation."

In The VIPs' apartment in Wildwood, when you walked into our kitchen/living room, displayed on the back wall was a sign that read "Beef," with an arrow pointing to the right bedroom, and "Conversation," with an arrow pointing to the bedroom on the left. Between Joey and me, whoever doesn't have a date that night sleeps on the sofa in the living room.

As it turns out, I will have a summer romance with one of the Follies girls. Her name is Gigi. No, really, I'm serious.

Most nights Joey is on the sofa.

Gerry and Joel's bedroom on the left remains true to its promise of conversation.

I tell Mr. Gable, "Thank you, but I will see you in September."

Once I start pharmacy school, Joe hires me to work with him in his dad's pharmacy. Joe's grandfather, who everyone calls "Pop," is then at least ninety years old and can't hear or see very well. Pop works behind the old-fashioned marble counter at the front of the store, making sodas and selling cigarettes and cigars.

One afternoon Joe and I are taking a break from filling prescriptions, standing and drinking a soda near the front. As we chat, one of the locals comes into the store and walks straight to the counter. "Hey, Pop, gimme a pack of Winstons."

Pop looks up, squints, and replies, "Vhat do you vant, Camels or Luckies?"

"Neither," the local answers.

Pop slams his fist down on the marble counter and yells back, "God dem it, come back vhen you decide!"

The guy walks out of the store, mumbling and scratching his head.

Joe and I laugh so hard we pee our pants.

(IV)
WHAT WAS I THINKING?

CHAPTER 13

My Sons' Mom

IT'S ON A blind date in 1962 when I first meet Lois. She is petite, pretty, and dark-haired. At the time she is seventeen and a senior at Bartram High School, and I am a nineteen-year-old sophomore at Temple University. While we're dating, both Lois and I continue to live at home with our parents.

I am not sure if I am more attracted to Lois or to her family. Whenever I visit, there are usually wonderful home-cooked meals, and that amazing aroma of something baking or roasting seems to embrace me when I enter her home. Laughter is always present as is a huge amount of hugging. Her grandmother, who is frequently there, reminds me of my bubbe.

Lois's home is a modest row house in West Philadelphia. I have since moved out of Plymouth Meeting and now live with my mom in an apartment in Northeast Philadelphia. Without a father at home and my mother working full time, I basically raised myself and was always given unlimited independence. Lois, on the other hand, grew up with both parents. Her dad, Len, is truly one of the kindest people I have ever met. Lois's mother, Sylvia, is an excellent cook and an overly involved parent whose personality I can best describe this way:

The difference between a neurotic and a psychotic is that a neurotic builds castles in the sky while a psychotic lives in them.

Sylvia cleans them!

Sylvia basically directs and controls Lois's life.

Eventually, married with two sons, Lois would seek to reclaim her independence.

Lois and I marry in June 1967. It is the thing to do when you think you have found the person with whom you want to spend the rest of your life, and you are too young to know absolutely anything about one of the most important decisions you will ever make. We are still children at the time. Lois is twenty-one, and I am twenty-three.

After Lois graduates from Bartram High School, she goes to work for Dr. Julius Newman, a center city Philadelphia ENT (ear, nose and throat) doctor who would go on to reinvent his career as a plastic surgeon known by the media as "Dr. Nose". Lois is his sole employee at this time. He teaches her audiometric analysis (hearing testing) and office management. Lois's business curriculum in high school prepares her well for the secretarial and professional duties that are required of her. When she leaves work in 1969, eight months pregnant with our first son, Josh, Dr. Nose replaces her with three employees.

Our first apartment at BrynMawr and Wynnefield avenues in West Philadelphia has one bedroom and is cozy and tastefully decorated, thanks to the money we received as wedding gifts. The large, black-and-white hounds tooth sofa sits atop a raspberry-colored carpet. A wall unit of walnut shelves houses my books and a stereo system. Our bedroom is filled wall-to-wall with a Mediterranean bedroom set resting on a light blue carpet.

When Josh is born, his crib occupies a tiny corner in our bedroom. This initial coziness eventually turns into really cramped quarters.

As a full-time student at Temple's School of Pharmacy, I am supplementing my income from playing in the band with working as a pharmacy student at Green's Pharmacy, located in the middle of the low-income projects in North Philly. The massive store has aisles of over-the-counter products, candy, and cigarettes on the street level. A guard stands watch at the front door, and two middle-aged women work the register located in the rear. The small pharmacy area is elevated at the back of the store and isolated from the endless traffic

in the front. Green's hourly wage for a pharmacy student is way better than any other pharmacy in the area. This is due to the fact that
the store is in the worst neighborhood imaginable, and even though
it is illegal, the owner takes nights off by having students man the
pharmacy.

On a night that would turn out to change the direction of my life, I
am working alone in the pharmacy. It's getting near closing time, and
the other student who was working with me left about thirty minutes
ago.

Earlier in the evening, a local gang kid had a run-in with one
of the register ladies who said to the boy, "Do you want to pay for
that candy you just put in your pocket?" The hoodlum replied, "You
wanna make me?" and was ushered out by the guard at the front. Two
hours later the kid returns with a handgun and pops two shots at the
guard. Crack! Crack! His bullets fortunately miss their target as he
runs out of the store.

In the elevated pharmacy, I am filling a line of welfare prescriptions, minding my own business, when I hear the sounds of gunfire.
Instinctively I immediately drop to the floor. Shaking from every part
of my body, I reach up from the cold tile underneath me and grab
the wall phone. My trembling fingers are just barely able to dial the
police.

When I stand up, there is a bullet visible in the wall behind me.

It measures eleven inches from the top of my head.

CHAPTER 14

Meeting Len

NOT WANTING TO worry Lois, I don't tell her what happened at work last night. Today I answer a newspaper ad for a pharmacy student. The store, Wakeling Apothecary, is directly across from Frankford Hospital in Philadelphia. Instead of aisles of non-health-care products, the store is all professional pharmacy and medical supplies. The classical music that plays in the background and the navy-colored carpeting make this place seem like a resort compared to the war zone where I was working yesterday.

The owner is a handsome and affable man wearing a clean white pharmacist jacket. He appears to be about ten years older than I and could pass for my older brother if I had been so blessed. Something clicks immediately between us, and he puts his arm around my shoulder when I tell him that I know nothing about the medical supply part of the store.

"Don't worry," he says, "I'll teach you." After a short interview, he hires me.

That pharmacist turns out to be my mentor, Leonard Abramson, who will go on to found US Healthcare where I eventually become senior vice president of sales and marketing. As a publicly held company, US Healthcare becomes the most successful managed health-care enterprise in the country and will be acquired by Aetna in 1996 for $8.9 billion. Len will walk away with $1 billion, the Gulfstream G4 airplane, a multimillion-dollar contract, and all the paper clips he can take. Thanks to Len, twenty-eight of US Healthcare's senior managers will receive five-year contracts with Aetna.

Later, long after the dust has settled, many people who like to count other people's money believe that I too must be extremely wealthy. My reply to them is, "I'm not greedy. All I wish I had is ten percent of what you think I have. If I did, I would be in fat city."

The running joke that Len and I share between us as we experience successes throughout our business lives together is "Not bad for a pharmacist."

In the next few months, between filling prescriptions, Len teaches me how to fit all types of orthopedic appliances, everything I need to know about durable medical equipment (DME), and the new federal health program for seniors: Medicare.

One day I walk into the store after school, and Len tells me that he is making a change. "I'm closing the pharmacy part of the store and making it all DME, orthopedic appliances, and medical supplies," he announces. "What will I be doing?" I ask. He smiles his "Len" grin, which resembles something between a Cheshire cat and the Dalai Lama, and then says, "I'm opening a second store in South Philadelphia, and you're going to run it."

As it turns out I do just that. The new store's hours coincide with my availability after school and on Saturday.

The name for the business is changed to Medical Equipment Unlimited (MEU), and a few months later, Len sells MEU to Spectro Industries. At this time in 1968, Spectro is a publicly traded company and the third largest drug wholesaling company in the country.

During my third year of pharmacy school, I become vice president of Medical Equipment Unlimited, division of Spectro Industries. Because of the exceptional profitability of MEU compared to the meager margins of the wholesale drug business, Len and I are the fair-haired boys in the company. This position of honor is challenged one Saturday morning when I open the mail and call Len at home to tell him about the letter from Medicare.

"Len, they are canceling home whirlpool baths as a covered DME item." I have no idea how he will respond, because the rental payments from the several hundred home whirlpools we have placed with arthritic patients account for almost fifty percent of our revenue.

"Don't worry, I have an idea. I'll tell you about it on Monday," he replies. Len's brilliant plan is to create an MEU national franchise program to place pharmacists into the surgical supply and home care business. Without getting into the specifics of how we did it (I will explain it all in my next book, *The Twenty Point Program*), we literally make it up as we go along and develop a very successful business that starts with the five Spectro wholesale drug locations in Philadelphia, Baltimore, Washington, DC, and Springfield and Worcester, Massachusetts. From there we expand to "master franchises" with other drug wholesalers that include McKesson and Robbins in New York, Florida, and Nassau; John B. Daniels in Atlanta; Zahn Drug in Chicago; and Bangor Drug in Maine.

With a radical increase in my income, Lois and I move from our cramped apartment into a three-bedroom row house in the Wynnefield Heights section of Philadelphia. It's 1970 and the purchase price of our home is eighteen thousand, five hundred dollars.

A year later our second son, Noah, is born.

On the surface, everything couldn't be better.

CHAPTER 15

A Bizarre Decision

MY BUSINESS TRAVELS take me on frequent trips all over the country and once a month to South Florida, where Len and I have developed a base of Medical Equipment Unlimited Franchisees. Lois stays home in our house in Philadelphia with the kids. With no car and no license to drive, she is dependent upon her parents, who live nearby, for transportation when I'm not there. As busy as I am with my work, I never realize how frustrating it must be for her.

In the winter of 1971, Len and I attend a conference on prepaid health care in New York City that is sponsored by the Practicing Law Institute. The audience consists of three hundred lawyers and two pharmacists.

I am sure that the lawyers are wondering, "Who the hell are these guys and what are they doing here?"

We take copious notes at the seminar, and afterward Len outlines a game plan for starting a new type of health plan called a health maintenance organization (HMO).

Later that year Len leaves Spectro to start the first HMO in Pennsylvania, Family Medical Centers, which morphs into HMO Pennsylvania and ultimately US Healthcare.

I remain at Spectro and am promoted to president of Medical Equipment Unlimited. As events unfold, it will be fourteen years before I again see or hear from Len.

Two years after my promotion, one of my franchisees, partners who own four pharmacies in South Florida, makes me an offer to join them and expand their surgical supply/home care business. This is all I need to push me over the edge to make a decision to leave Spectro and the cold weather up north and move to the paradise of South Florida. Like other life-changing decisions I make on the fly, this is a knee-jerk reaction that involves no investigation, no thought about consequences, and absolutely no discussion with anyone else, including my wife.

Looking back I realize how truly bizarre that choice was in the context of my marriage. I hadn't consulted with Lois and had unilaterally opted to move our family to a strange place and uproot her from the security of her parents.

If Wikipedia were around then, and you searched for "Really Big Asshole," the first thing that would pop up is a picture of me.

As it eventually evolves, this turns out to be the best move for both of us.

But first we will both go through a lot of pain and true hardship.

CHAPTER 16

Phoenix Rising

IT IS 1973. Lois remains distant and uninterested about any decision regarding the move. At some point on a business trip to Florida, I purchase a new home in Coral Springs. While the house is being finished, I move down by myself and live in a hotel for two months. Finally, once construction is complete, Lois, Josh, and baby Noah join me.

During this time I start working with my new business partners. It doesn't take me long to confirm what I have suspected from the beginning: the people with whom I have entered into business are shams of individuals and have no money to advance a new enterprise. Less than six months later I leave my partners and start my own business, Health Care Services, Inc., with a twenty-five thousand dollar loan from the Small Business Administration. My dire financial condition places additional stress on our marriage.

In the first three years in Florida, our financial and marital lives are on parallel death spirals. Lois and I are each going through self-actualization in our own ways and eventually realize that we have irreconcilably grown apart. Our marriage is devoid of emotion. Lois's animosity for my uncaring and unthinking decisions has turned into total indifference.

She joins a women's consciousness-raising group after being encouraged by some of her friends. It is there that she gains the awareness to understand her feelings and the strength to do something about them.

The husbands of the seven women in Lois's group are urged by their wives to form their own group. Initially, wanting only to appease our wives, we reluctantly agree, and in 1976 we form our own men's consciousness-raising group.

Our first sessions are more about telling personal stories and complaining about our wives than expressing anything remotely resembling a feeling. After three or four weeks of this nonsense, we agree that although this is fun, it's a waste of time the way we are going about it. We decide to lay down some ground rules that will help make our Thursday night meetings more meaningful. The following are the "rules" to which we agree:

There will be a specific topic for each week's session.

The focus of our meetings will be on our feelings, and that week's topic will serve as the centerpiece for those feelings.

Whoever is hosting that week's session is responsible for creating and announcing that week's topic.

The group is a safe place to say anything you want.

No one is allowed to challenge your thoughts or feelings.

Whatever is said at one of our meetings stays inside our group.

Some examples of our weekly topics are:

"My Feelings About My Marriage"

"How I See My Role as a Parent"

"How, I Believe, People Think of Me"

"How I Perceive Masculinity and Femininity"

While the six of us who remain in the group have zero expectations from the experience, along the way we uncover something most unexpected. We discover ourselves.

We find out that we aren't alone in some of our thoughts. My most liberating revelation is that I'm not "weird." It is most comforting to know that other men also have feelings and can share them. Our men's consciousness-raising group becomes such a safe place to open up that, after six months of our getting together, the youngest guy, John, who had been married less than a year, announces one night that he is gay.

This is the late seventies, and the attitude toward nontraditional lifestyles is much less accepting than what it will become years later. In spite of the time period, when the words come out of John's mouth, none of us expresses anything but acceptance for him.

"OK, so what else is new, John?" is kind of the response.

John cries, and we all hug him.

This is certainly my first excursion into self-awareness and intro-spection. For me the most empowering part of our meetings, which last over a year, is my realization that there is so much more to me than the façade of the individual I present to others. I always believed that I was a good person, but through my consciousness-raising group, I start to really like myself by gaining a whole new perspective and relationship with my inner self.

I have come a long way from being that little boy who cowered in the corner as he watched his father, in a drunken tirade, slam his mother against the wall; the little boy who vowed to himself never to express anger; the little boy who never shared any feelings with his mother out of fear that he would upset her; the little boy who always felt like he was on the outside looking in.

Coming from no awareness about anything emotional to getting in touch with my deepest feelings, I too am faced with the fact that my marriage to Lois has wound down to nothing. It turns out that she can tolerate the wasteland of our living together less than I. It is Lois who announces to me one day that she is moving out. She has decided to leave me in the house to raise our sons. For the first time in her life, she needs to be on her own. Being a full-time mother is no longer part of her plan.

We go to one lawyer and have him draw up a simple agreement.

I will be the custodial parent and stay in our home with the boys.

She will have visitation at least twice a month on weekends at her apartment.

At our divorce hearing, the judge asks me if I want her to pay me child support.

I respectfully decline.

The day that Lois moves out of the house turns out to be as emotionless as our marriage had become. We prepared the kids for what is about to happen. Josh and Noah will see their mom on alternate weekends, and they will have their own room at her apartment.

The driver and truck from my business come to our house to carry Lois's things to her new home. Before moving day, we divided our furniture, pictures, and dishes. Today everyone helps pack the truck. There are no tears as Josh and Noah wave good-bye when their mom drives off.

It is June 1977, exactly ten years since we were married.

(V)
STEIN BOYS AND FRIENDS

CHAPTER **17**

Ground Rules

ONCE LOIS LEAVES, it's important for me to let Josh and Noah know that the three of us are now a team and that we have to support each other. Responsibility is essential, and we discuss that even though Josh is only seven and Noah five, each one of us has an important role.

Mine is to go to work every day and make our lives financially stable. For my sons it is going to school and doing their best. Each of us has to share in household chores.

We then agree to one overarching rule that is essential to our major roles:

No one gets sick.

Surprisingly, in the almost nine years the three of us resided in Florida under this arrangement, no one was ever sick enough to prevent my going to work or their going to school.

Throughout this time and afterward, people would comment how tough raising two sons by myself must have been for me. My response has always been that it was one of the best times in my life and, regardless of whatever happened, everything always just worked out.

I also state, "As kind, introspective, and compassionate as my daughter, Alexandra, is, if I had two girls instead of two boys, the daily drama that rears its ugly head in preteen females would have taken its toll on me, and I probably would have killed myself."

The real difficulties of these years emanate from the unexpressed thoughts and feelings of each of the Stein boys.

Both Josh and Noah will take a long time, if ever, to reconcile the motivations for their mother's leaving and the profound hurt that remains. In addition, each will never forget my sometimes anger, frustration, and irrational behavior from events in my life that I stupidly and unthinkingly directed at them. The pain that I carry around today stems from my, at times, less than exemplary behavior during that period.

A good analogy is when it was publicized years ago that Audi cars had sudden acceleration. That event negated all of the positive years for the Audi brand. In an instant, years of favorable experience are eradicated. Only a glaring negative remains, and it is front and center. Similarly all of the wonderful memories and sharing of positive emotional experiences with my boys are sometimes occluded by memories of outbursts for which I had to apologize.

One of the basic tenets of a Jewish mother is the use of guilt as a social weapon. Jewish guilt is that feeling a mother instills in her kids because they do not meet her irrational expectations.

In my case, I own all the guilt and lay it all on myself.

CHAPTER **18**

The Father Becomes the Fodder

ONE OF THE people I meet in my travels is Gary Stein (no relationship), a newspaper writer who is doing an article on single parents. I become his "fodder" on two occasions. Below are quotes from both articles.

Excerpt of an article that appeared in the February 4, 1979 edition of *The Miami Herald*, written by Gary Stein:

He Has Custody of the Kids?
Establishing Responsibility a Major Role of Single Dads

...Mel Stein, 36, realized he couldn't do it all himself. "I realized I was like a slave so we sat down and talked about sharing in the daily tasks."

...In order to maintain his business and the household, Stein has placed his boys in an after-school day care center. "It's not a place I'm really happy about," Stein said. But for the time being it is the best compromise he can make.

..."They know my love is unconditional," Stein said of his children. "We can get mad at each other about stuff, but the stuff is not bigger than our love. I think men are emotionally deprived. They are not allowed to be emotional. Since I got in touch with my feelings, life has been much more enjoyable. The neat thing about knowing what you are feeling," he added, "is that you can get off it. You can go back to being happy again."

...Some children pressure their fathers into new relationships—even sexual relationships. "One nine-year-old asked me, 'Why don't you sleep with my mommy?' I was completely shocked," one father said. Stein's children were equally direct. "I never had a friend sleep over," said Stein. "Then one week Josh asked, 'Hey, Dad, why don't you have friends sleep over? Noah and I have friends sleep over.' Well, the next week a friend slept over."

...When Mel Stein first became a single dad, he checked in on Noah's kindergarten class to make sure his son was adapting well to school. Noah's teacher told Stein not to worry. It seems a little girl in Noah's class came to school in tears because her parents were getting divorced. "Noah put his arm around her and told his friend, 'It's going to be OK'," Stein reminisced.

Excerpt from the June 17, 1983 issue of the *Fort Lauderdale News*, written by Gary Stein:

Father's Day message of love to the kids

The thing I really love about this book Mel Stein has been putting together for seven years is that he doesn't care if it ever gets published.

My kind of author.

"It's more of a journal than anything else," said Stein (no relation). "If I never get it published, at least I've documented a piece of me. It's something my kids can see."

Stein has tentatively titled his tome *The Making of a Dad: Growing Up with Joshua and Noah*. Perhaps he could have titled it *Diary of a Father of the '80s*, because in a lot of ways that is what Mel Stein is. Thirty nine years old and divorced for six years ("I'm still very good friends with my ex-wife"), the

Coral Springs resident took custody of his two kids when the marriage broke up. And ever since then, Stein has been putting his feelings and emotions onto paper as he writes about what it's like to be a single father and raise a couple of kids.

"When I was eight years old, my mom worked," he smiled. "I made dinner and cleaned the house. Now, I'm doing it again."

"I used to read the 'how-to' books, and the author would always give me a laundry list of things to do that I couldn't relate to. The only things I can relate to are experiences," which is what his journal is all about.

Like writing about the first time he brought a woman home. Or writing down his thoughts on taking his kid to school for the first time. Or writing about his reaction the day Josh cut a class. "I had to tell him he did something wrong," Stein said, "but I also told him I loved him. I never had that as a kid."

"Sometimes I know I have to do something as a father, and I don't know exactly what to do, so we wing it," added Stein, who is general manager of National Convalescent Aids in Fort Lauderdale. He is also a drummer who works weddings and bar mitzvahs, and was an extra in the flick *Caddyshack*.

"Yeah, I think being a father today is different. I think people are more in touch with their humanness now. In our parents' generation, people were into economic survival. Now we have more time to think about ourselves and our relationships.

"I don't find being a single parent restricting at all. I find it nourishing, supportive. I learn something from my kids every day, and I can be totally me with my sons. I can get upset and yell, and I know they'll still love me."

That attitude of coexistence explains a little about why, on this Father's Day, Stein is making this latest notation in his journal for Josh, 14, and Noah, 11:

"I'm really glad I'm your dad! You have supported me in what I do by being the responsible people you've become. You have helped nurture and preserve the little boy in me. You have helped me to understand that I was not Superdad and, more importantly, that I didn't have to be.

...now, on this Father's Day, I want you both to know how much I love you."

CHAPTER 19

First Time Away

IT'S SUNDAY MORNING and in a little while Lois and I will be driving Josh and Noah to the airport for a visit with their grandparents in Philadelphia. Yesterday I took them for a haircut and then to Sears for new clothes—pants, shirts, shoes, and socks. Last night they each tried on their new outfits at least three times, and this morning they were dressed by 7:30 a.m., even though the flight from Fort Lauderdale to Philadelphia isn't until 1:45 p.m. They are super excited about the trip and more than ready for this first time away by themselves. Maybe this is in part to how terrific they both look.

It's been only a month since Lois and I separated. We remain friends, and we both agreed that it would be best for the boys if we said good-bye to them together. They will be away the next two weeks, and I have been anticipating my feelings of loneliness until they return. Josh shared with me last night how he was feeling about his trip—excited about being the big brother and watching out for both himself and Noah. He also said that he was a little nervous about the trip and being away from home.

Most meaningful for me was Josh's proclaiming, "Don't worry, Dad, Noah and I will be all right."

That conversation was an eye-opener for me, because I can never recall expressing any feelings to my mom or anyone else as I grew up. I was such a solitary person and had zero training from anyone regarding the existence, acknowledgment, or articulation of feelings. The only remembrance I have that has any similarity to the discussion of an emotion is my mom's frequent use of the word "aggravation."

Although I always somewhat enjoyed being alone, I am also realizing at this moment that I am trying to talk myself into the fact that I might enjoy being alone for the next two weeks. I'm not sure if this is a major realization or if it is a bullshit rationalization.

Maybe it's a little of both.

At least just my asking that question is a hell of a long way from where my head was two years ago. For me, gaining some self-awareness and introspection is really a double-edged sword. I like myself a lot more, but I am now totally responsible for the events of my life. There is no blame or accountability that I can lay off on others. It is all up to me.

Lois and I are taking Josh and Noah to the airport today. Josh was afraid last night about the flight itself. I felt like a real dad, both by reassuring him and holding him close and also by understanding how much he needed that reassurance and closeness to me.

My sons will be away for the next two weeks, and I know now that I will be fine.

I also know that sometimes it's really going to be lonely.

CHAPTER **20**

Thirty-Four

I WILL BE thirty-four in two weeks, September 27, 1977. This is really the first time I have thought about becoming thirty-four. That sounds like a strange number. I don't remember anyone I've ever known being thirty-four.

Last night I met a very traditional woman on a blind date. When I first saw her, I was struck by how different she looked from my usual potential girlfriends. Our phone conversation a few days before, although a bit formal, provided no indication of how she would be in person. She was dressed primly, and her hair was in a bun. Her whole demeanor screamed "prude," but I was willing to see where the evening's experience led.

With all my "awareness training," I tried to separate my first impression of her from the possibility of having an enjoyable evening.

It was really hard to do.

Have I changed so much?

I guess I am not so sure.

As it turned out, I was really annoyed by her manner. Maybe she truly wasn't into me and was just making small talk. Maybe she was exceptionally secretive or uncomfortable because she didn't know me well enough. Maybe it was all the above.

She was telling me a story, and I requested more information.

"I'm not quite sure I understand. Please explain the details, who you are talking about, so I can better appreciate what you are telling me."

"Oh, I can't tell you that" was her response.

"Why not?"

"Because it's personal."

"Are you kidding?" I thought. "Why even tell me the damn story?"

Sometimes I am very critical and judgmental. I don't like that about myself. I like to believe that I have become so aware and accepting of others and their opinions.

Maybe I am starting to not care if everyone likes me, or maybe I have just decided that it's all right for me to express my beliefs and just accept it as that.

Who knows?

Thirty-four.

CHAPTER 21

Rituals

WHILE MOST OF the time Josh, Noah, and I made it up as we went along day by day, we did establish and maintain several "rituals"' Whether they were weekly or annual occurrences was irrelevant. What was important was that we could count on them to happen.

Tevye said it best in *Fiddler*—one word—"Tradition!"

Candlelight Dinner

Once a week, on Wednesday evenings, we have a candlelight dinner with fresh flowers on the table. I set the table with our best dishes and glasses and fold the napkins so that they create pockets for the silverware. It is truly a special night that provides the three of us a chance to talk about what is happening in our lives and to air any concerns or conflicts. The meal consists of one of my famous "gourmet" dinners, usually a casserole of beans and franks or spaghetti and meatballs. One of my requests is that whatever I prepare is what we have for dinner - no exceptions or substitutions.

Noah has always been the most "not always accepting" when it comes to my cooking. One Wednesday early on after we started this ritual, Noah refuses to eat the dinner du jour I made and goes into his room to sulk. Josh and I finish the meal and are sitting on the sofa reading a story when the first sighting of Noah occurs since his disappearance at dinner.

Looking up from the book, I see Noah pop his head in from the kitchen. He is holding a can of Chef Boyardee spaghetti and meatballs and has that sorrowful, please-help-me look in his eyes. The underlying fact is that he is five years old and doesn't know how to open the can. I look at Josh and painfully struggle to control the smile that is straining to appear on my face. At this moment I am in a real conflict. Do I take a hard line, or do I break my rules and provide sustenance to the forlorn little boy staring at me?

After agonizing for what seems like an hour, but is actually about a minute, my heart melts, and the Jewish mother in me vaults from the sofa to feed the baby.

A frequent side dish for the meal is fresh corn on the cob, which Josh and I love. Every Wednesday I stop at a local farm stand for corn that is picked that day. Later I'll boil it just enough to be warm and crunchy. Noah is always reluctant to try new foods. Corn, if not at the bottom, is very low on his list. I accept the fact that for the foreseeable future Noah is not going to try the corn, but Josh and I will not stop discussing how unbelievably spectacular the corn is.

After months of this weekly discourse and affirmation of the attributes of corn, Noah's stoic attitude about corn starts to erode. One night he slides a piece on his plate, hoping no one will notice. He won't give us the satisfaction of agreeing that the corn is delicious, but he devours every morsel and from that moment forward he is addicted.

After that breakthrough I never give Noah an "I told you so," but I still delight in the fact that Josh and I converted him.

He is one stubborn kid.

The Stockings Were Hung on the Drum Set with Care

We are Jewish and preserving the traditions of a Jewish home has been important to me since my early school days at Beth Jacob. Although we go to services at synagogue on the High Holy Days, Rosh Hashanah, the Jewish New Year, and Yom Kippur, the Day of Atonement, we always celebrate Passover and Hanukkah in our home. The eight nights of Hanukkah are always special, because each night at sundown Josh and Noah stand next to me, my arms around each of their shoulders, as we sing the prayers in Hebrew and then light the candles in the menorah. Once the blessings are recited and the candles are lit, they each receive their nightly gift.

As important as Hanukkah is in our home, Christmas morning has its own distinction. Hanukkah frequently coincides with Christmas, and although we don't have a Christmas tree, I do have presents for Josh and Noah on Christmas morning.

These Christmas presents are in addition to the presents they receive for Hanukkah—one each night for the eight days of the holiday. It seems that I am continually barely making ends meet financially, so the presents are never elaborate. There is usually one important present—something my sons really want—and the rest of the gifts are mostly necessities like clothes, socks, books, or school supplies. Every gift is wrapped in special paper and ribbon or bows, which I save and reuse each year. When I run out of paper or a quick wrap is required, I discover that tin foil is a wonderful alternative. Although everyone else in the western hemisphere may already be aware of this utility of tin foil, for Mr. Suzy Homemaker, this is a revelation.

In the corner of our family room, across from the white, lacquered, wall-to-ceiling bookshelves and stereo is my drum set, which I frequently play to the music from my favorite Motown or jazz recordings. My drum set, a thirty-year-old, gold sparkle WFL (William F. Ludwig) with Zildian cymbals, is like an old friend to me. These are the same drums that I played throughout college with various dance bands and later with The VIPs. My drums have been there with me at numerous fraternity parties at Temple University and the University of Pennsylvania. At Penn's "Spring Fling," The VIPs were the featured band, and my drums were set up in The Quad for our afternoon performance. They are the drums that sat in the middle of the stage at concerts where I played with a golf glove on each hand and, because of The VIPs' superlative volume, actually broke aluminum drumsticks during the performance. They were miked at recording studios and were there at Swan Records in South Philadelphia when The VIPs recorded our "smash hit," "Would You Believe" in 1967. I played these drums when The VIPs worked with Bobby Rydell in Wildwood, New Jersey; with Chubby Checker; and later with Lee Andrews and the Hearts. These same drums paid my way for eight years of college and later helped save my house from foreclosure by the Small Business Administration (see Chapter 30). My drums are truly a large part of my life, and they now serve proudly as the repository for Christmas presents.

Yes, even though we are Jewish and celebrate Hanukkah for eight nights, Christmas morning is a time that provides a "bonus" ritual to share with my kids.

The reality is that we don't have a fireplace or mantel.

The solution is that every Christmas Eve the stockings are hung on the drum set with care.

Whether for Hanukkah or Christmas, Josh and Noah are always appreciative of whatever they receive—except when they open those "soft" packages, which are usually a six-pack of socks or underwear. In addition Santa always manages to leave a gift or two for me. I always amaze myself how surprised I am when I open the same gifts on Christmas morning that I just wrapped the night before. Sometimes Josh leaves notes for Santa, even though he tries to make them look like Noah wrote them:

From Josh but addressed, "Note from Noah":

Dear Santa, please have my dad wake me and my lovingful brother (Josh) in the morning, and please wish Josh my blessings.

And another offering from Josh:

Dear Santa, Merry Christmas and here's your midnight snack. It's just a few of Robyn's (my girlfriend) cookies; your milk is in the refrigerator. I've been good. By the way, Santa, please get

Josh his super-action controller. I'm getting sick of him worrying about it. Get Dad something nice too.

Well, Merry Christmas, Santa. Talk to you later. Happy New Year!

Love, Noah

After the opening of the presents, I prepare my special pancakes, the same ones that I make frequently on Sunday mornings. Then I turn up the stereo to stadium volume, and with the Disney Electric Light Parade blaring, I dance around the house with alternately Josh and then Noah on my shoulders.

Tradition—it's a wonderful thing!

High Holiday Services

We lived in Coral Springs, Florida, which unlike the probably two hundred thousand plus citizens who live there now, had about five thousand when we were there. Although there were several churches in town, there was no synagogue. A Jewish congregation met in the community center, and I purchased two prayer books, *Gates of Repentance*, for my sons and me to share when we attended Rosh Hashanah and Yom Kippur services.

Neither Josh nor Noah is an enthusiastic attendee or an active participant, but once there they behave like gentlemen. Although we never discuss it, I like to believe that they know how important this is to me. I always consider their good behavior at temple their gift to me.

When Josh is twelve years old, I have the rabbi come to our home to give him bar mitzvah lessons. The rabbi leaves recorded tapes of Josh's Torah portion, which Josh listens to and memorizes. At his bar mitzvah, Josh recites by rote the incantations from the rabbi's tapes. Noah cannot stop beaming at his brother. It is the proudest I have ever seen him. Afterward Lois and her parents, my mom, and a handful of friends come back to our house for a celebration. Lunch is catered by Merle, one of my former girlfriends, who has a catering business. The Marty Lacks Band provides the music with me on the drums.

The sad part of this remembrance is that I never give Noah the same opportunity to have a bar mitzvah. There are a million excuses that I can conjure up for this omission. I am too busy; I have no money; I am depressed and just can't get it together. The bottom line is that this is one tradition that is really important to my son, and I let him down. Even though Noah makes no request or mention about having a bar mitzvah at this point, years later he will tell me about his disappointment.

In this instance I am ashamed that I let my son down.

I am also disappointed in myself for not living up to my own expectations of being a good dad.

Annual Vacation to Disneyworld

Each year on spring break, we vacation for a week at Disneyworld in Orlando, Florida. The trip itself is a three and a half hour drive from Coral Springs and always, inevitably, proves eventful.

I must digress a bit and let you know that I have spent a lot of time as a single parent taking various self-awareness trainings. These include est (Ehrhard Seminar Training—Werner Ehrhard's cultish forums), consciousness-raising groups, PET (Parent Effectiveness Training), and tai chi (studying with a master in the park in Fort Lauderdale). For those of you who now might be thinking that I am a bit strange, I will tell you that in my est training and seminars, there definitely were some people who would worship cottage cheese if it were presented to them as the light, the way, and the truth. In fact, in every discipline that requires introspection, there exists an element of those who are "off the wall" blind followers. On the other hand, I like to think that I have taken only those aspects of each discipline that were applicable to me and used them to enhance my living and parenting experience.

So here I am, all the tools of awareness and parenting in my hip pocket, setting out on a little drive to Orlando with Josh and Noah seated in the back. The first half hour of the drive is always great: exciting and engaging discussion about what we will do at Disneyworld, joking with each other, singing songs, and playing road games.

It always fascinates me how quickly things can turn south. I'm not sure how it eventually starts, but it's like a tropical storm that keeps building strength until it becomes a full-blown hurricane. "That's my book." "No, it's mine." "Josh hit me." "Noah hit me first." Out of nowhere a pleasant car ride is transformed into hysteria: fighting, yelling, and totally out-of-control feelings. What I do know, as sure as God made little green apples, is that all the est, all the psychology, and all the PET goes out the window.

"Just let me get my hand back there and grab something!"

As it turns out, I just mete out the discipline du jour as warranted. Once I actually stop the car on the side of the road for thirty minutes until the mayhem from the backseat subsides, and Josh and Noah realize that we are not going anywhere until they get their acts together. At some point the storm passes, and eventually we arrive at Disneyworld and settle in.

The best part of our trip always is the reality that once we arrive, we are all kids in the Magic Kingdom.

I don't do spinning or flipping rides well, and I never let my kids go on a ride without me. Mr. Toad's Wild Ride, Peter Pan, and It's a Small World are the limit of my speed. On one of our earlier trips, Noah begs me to go on the Space Mountain ride with him and Josh. After minutes of his encouragement and pleading about how it will be fine, I reluctantly agree. Noah and I sit together in the front car, and Josh sits by himself directly behind us. It only takes about thirty seconds into the ride for me to realize that this was not a good decision on my part. After what seems like eternity, the ride ends, and I stumble off, dizzy and nauseated. Finding the nearest bench to sit, I plunk myself down. With my head buried in my hands, I mutter, "I am going to sit here for the next two hours. Please don't go too far, and stay close to each other. Make sure you come back then."

This experience makes me understand how some people can actually say, "Dear Lord, please take me." If it weren't for my boys, I would have asked to be taken right there.

In April 1982 Josh uses some of his bar mitzvah money to purchase a new bicycle, which gives him the freedom to ride to the Coral Springs Mall and meet his friends. Two weeks later he leaves the mall to return home and discovers that his new Schwinn is not there. It has been stolen, and he calls me, heartbroken, to pick him up. We stop at the police station to report the theft. For Josh, this is a cruel lesson in being responsible and, in this case, locking his bicycle. Unfortunately it is never recovered, but a few weeks later, on our annual trip to the Magic Kingdom, something truly magical actually happens.

We are staying at a Holiday Inn in Kissimmee, Florida, and Easter Sunday is the next day. There is to be an Easter egg hunt, and prizes will be awarded for finding special plastic eggs with prize notes inside. The next morning, after a pancake breakfast, Josh and Noah join the legion of kids wandering the grounds around the Holiday Inn pool, searching for eggs and surprises. It takes about forty-five minutes for Josh to come screaming back to me after finding one of the special eggs. Noah and I are as excited as Josh, but it isn't until we open the egg that we discover that Josh had hit the jackpot with his find.

The note inside reads, "Congratulations, you have won the grand prize: a new bicycle."

The Tooth Fairy

After Lois moves out, I discover that note writing is a wonderful way to acknowledge and encourage my kids. This is accomplished through informal letters that the Tooth Fairy leaves my kids after they lose a tooth. As a point of reference, when Noah was four years old, I let my facial hair grow, and I had a full beard for the next eight years. Always accompanying the Tooth Fairy's signature is a bearded face sitting on a tooth.

April 9, 1978
Dear Josh,

I can't believe this terrific tooth. It is really delicious! You sure caught me by surprise. I happened to be in Pittsburgh when your tooth came out, and I had to run back to Coral Springs. It's always good to see you and your neat room.

The next time I see you I'm hoping your report card will be better.
I love you,
The Tooth Fairy

November 29, 1978
Dear Tooth Fairy,
I lost my tooth today. I would like a note and some money too.
Love,
Noah
Thank you.

The Tooth Fairy responds:

Dear Noah,
My! What a pleasant surprise to have such a beautiful tooth and to get it so close to your birthday. It really is good to see you again. It has been a long time since I visited the Steins. Noah, I think Ruby gave you a terrific haircut. Also I know your dad is really annoying sometimes about straightening your room, but I want you to know that your room looks so much better clean; and it must be a real pleasure for you to walk into a fresh, clean room and be able to find things you are looking for. I am very proud of how you have been helping your dad around the house. I want you to know that he really appreciates your help and that it upsets him when he has to beg for it. He loves you and brother Josh more than anything, and what he really wants is for you and Josh to be prepared for the world not only for now but also for when you get older. I know that you have been getting better organized with your schoolwork and that you will be getting

better grades. Your life can be as wonderful as you make it. Studying and being organized in school is a great start. Keep up the good work.

I guess I wrote you a lot this trip because I probably won't see you again for a long time.

Well, it's been real swell. Say hello to bro Josh and to your dad for me. I love you all very much!!!

The Tooth Fairy

The following note is written by Josh and left on Noah's bed the next day to respond to Noah's tooth loss. It is both an attempt by Josh to usurp the power of the Tooth Fairy and an expression of his unspoken feelings about his alligator:

Dear Noah,

I heard you lost your tooth yesterday. It was very pretty. It was the best tooth I ever saw. I hear Joshua's alligator died yesterday. It was so sad that I was crying.

Love,

The Tooth Fairy

Following this note is not a picture of the true, bearded Tooth Fairy. Instead there is a picture of well-drawn fairy princess with the caption:

This is what I really look like.

Sometimes Josh or Noah write back to the Tooth Fairy and, like me, express feelings, which sometimes are manifestations of their repressed anger and frustrations:

January 12, 1979

Dear TF,

Why don't you ever give me money!? I mean like three to

five dollars instead of one dollar in pennies—wow. I spend a hard time pulling out these teeth, so I expect big bucks. Why do all the other kids get at least five dollars in *cash*, and all I get is a dollar in change? What are you, a cheapskate? Why do you rip me off? If you don't give me big bucks, I'll just keep ripping out my teeth till I have no more teeth to pull.
From Josh
PS: I know you're the TF, Dad.

May 4, 1980, 11:30 p.m.
I just walked into my bedroom after coming home from a date. There's a note on my bed. It's in Noah's writing:

Dear Dad, my tooth fell out.

I had just kissed Noah good night before I went to sleep and had already found the little plastic bag under his pillow that he uses to package his infamous lost teeth.
The difference tonight is that all communication regarding prior tooth losses has been addressed to the Tooth Fairy—never a note addressed to Dad. The parent in me wells-up with sadness.
The end of the Tooth Fairy era?
Never!
The Tooth Fairy responds with this note I leave under Noah's pillow, along with a dollar offering for his precious molar:

Dear Noah,
Of all the houses I expected to visit tonight, yours definitely was not on my list. Please understand that I really do love to come and see you. It is just that I was surprised to see your molar come out. It's as excellent a tooth as I've seen from you. Thanks, it's delicious! Noah, I was glad to see better grades on your report card, your splendid performance in the fashion show, your being selected for the school play, and

the way you have been really helping your dad. I know that he knows how much you really love him and support him. Noah, why did you leave your dad a note about your tooth? I'm the one who always writes you and leaves you money, not him.

Come on, give me a break. I love you!
The Tooth Fairy

It saddens me that I am not the Tooth Fairy.

The Tooth Fairy always has time to communicate love and acknowledgment.

The Tooth Fairy is always appreciative and pragmatic.

The Tooth Fairy is a wonderful person.

I wish I could be like him all the time.

Monday Night Dinner—Picnics on the Beach

The best way to counter the cruel fact that the weekend has ended and that Monday means back to school and work is to make the beginning of the week a time for a special treat. Before picking up Josh and Noah from an after-school care center, I pack a picnic bag that usually includes sandwiches, chips, fresh fruit, and drinks. Then we go straight to the beach and, before dinner, play ball and Frisbee and run in the sand. We spread a large blanket on the sand, which gives us ample room to enjoy our dinner. It is always a great time to be pals away from the house.

During one of our beach nights, sitting on another blanket near where we are camped is a young mother with two teenage girls. We start talking, and the woman asks me what I do with my sons after school while I am still at work. I tell her about the after-school care center, which neither my boys nor I love but is the only solution I have. She suggests that her daughters would love to "babysit" after school. She can pick up my kids from school and take them to her house, which is about a mile from where we live. As it turns out, Josh and Noah really like these people a lot better than the after-school center, and this lady and her daughters become our solution for after-school care.

Whenever people ask me, "Isn't it hard for me to work and care for my sons?," my response is that everything seems to just work out, making it up as we go along, just like with these strangers we met on the beach.

It is never the physical arrangements that cause difficulty in my life as a single parent.

It is the emotional aspect that creates my stress and my shortcomings.

Rituals like Wednesday candlelight dinners, holidays, vacations, the Tooth Fairy, and Monday night beach picnics are the easy part. I am able to juggle all of the physical stuff in our lives and not only deal with it but also make it great fun for my sons and me.

Being there all the time emotionally for Josh and Noah is where I fail as a parent.

I am not there for myself.

How can I be there for them?

CHAPTER 22

Self-Discovery

ONE OF THE things I beat myself up about is being a hopeless romantic.

Today kids listen to songs like "Take It to the Head," "Cashin' Out," and "Outrageous." They watch movies such as *Scream*, *Saw*, and my all-time favorite, *Attack Of The Vegan Zombies*.

In the '50s I grew up watching Doris Day and Rock Hudson movies.

When I was fourteen, I saw Cary Grant and Deborah Kerr in *An Affair to Remember*, one of the greatest love stories of all time.

My formative years were spent listening to songs like "At Last" (my love has come along), "You Belong to Me," "Love Me Tender," and "The Glory of Love."

That was my training, and I have been programmed to be in love with the fantasy of love.

Now after reveling in a new love, I realize that it can never be as special as it is in the beginning—relating only on a romantic level with no other responsibility to the relationship. As that newness fades, what happens? Intellectually, a good relationship will get better with time, but I get uncomfortable when someone starts to get attached.

Is it that I am not ready to be close with someone again, or is that I just don't want to be in a committed relationship?

Is it that I simply haven't yet met "the one," or is it that I will never?

I have no clue at this point.

We are all like electrical charges traveling on a maze of circuitry that is our life. Sometimes at relay points, we merge with other electrical charges, and they travel with us long distances along the circuit. Sometimes they oppose each other like magnetic poles.

I watched a show on TV last night about the evolution of dinosaurs. One theory proposed that some dinosaurs were warm-blooded and that birds today are direct descendents. I miss the scientific process I learned in college and wish I had the appreciation then that I do now—the desire to learn for the sake of learning and not for a grade on an exam. As an undergraduate student, I was like a parrot capable of spouting the rote lessons I had been fed in my college classes. Never questioning anything. Never seeing any real overall plan or purpose to those teachings. Never truly understanding how anything was connected to the real world.

Seventy million years ago dinosaurs wandered the planet.

Seventy million years!

I now think about how long one year is and how much can change in that time.

The other day, after meeting a girl who was overly eager to dive into a relationship, I wrote the following:

"Please don't lean on me.

I need my space as much as you do yours.

Be a free person open to whatever life brings.

I am not ready to love again, so just be with me for the goodness you see in me and not for anything more.

Don't depend on me for your happiness, for I am the same as you with the same frailties and fears.

Let's just enjoy this moment in our lives and see where it takes us."

I intended to share my note with this girl, but I decided not to.

I just never called back.

CHAPTER **23**

Don't Label Me

WRITING IS TRULY my therapy and my release. Sometimes when I furiously scribble down my thoughts, it's like floodgates opening and relieving the uncontrollable pressure inside.

One of my dates the other night called me "deep." Maybe I am now, but up until a few years ago, I never saw any depth in myself beyond the façade I put on—the veneer of being what people wanted me to be.

I really am so different now.

Upon hearing that I am a single parent raising my two sons, the usual comment back from a woman I meet is, "I really give you a lot of credit. How do you do it?"

First of all, I really don't look at what I do as anything special. I don't need any acknowledgment from others for being a single parent. It is simply what I do, and I truly love it. It keeps me alive.

My boys are a constant source of energy and inspiration for me. They enable me to do a lot of things I probably would never do if I were alone—things like going to Disneyworld and G-rated movies, goofing around, and acting like a kid myself without feeling self-conscious about it.

What I would value being acknowledged for is the person I am. Before becoming a single parent, I never recall feeling this good about myself. Then, when I had no introspection, I was totally fine with being acknowledged for what I did and for my accomplishments. Now I want to be appreciated for being an honest, loving man who just happens to be raising his children.

I attempt to view life in the following context: A person with arthritis can be labeled "an arthritic," a person whose entire existence revolves around his arthritis—his frustrations, his limitations, his inability to cope at times because of a physical impairment. Or he could simply be a person who has an affliction called arthritis, but a person who is much bigger than his disease. The context of a person's life is either as an arthritic or as someone who enjoys life to its fullest and, by the way, happens to have a condition called arthritis that may restrict some physical activities.

Don't label me, please.

Labels put people in unfathomable places from which there are no escapes. To get beyond any labels and to be accepted and acknowledged as a caring and honorable person in the world today is truly attaining something special.

Who I am is not what I do.

What I do is simply one part of who I am.

I am bigger than what I do.

I am greater than the sum of all the things I do.

Who I am is my genetic makeup modified by all of my life's experiences.

I cease to grow as a person when any label places me in a category and holds me there in your mind.

So give me credit when I set a world record for something I have trained and practiced.

Give me credit when I perform a philanthropic act of immense proportion.

Thank me if I save someone's life.

But please, don't label me.

Just acknowledge me as a good man who happens to be raising his two children.

CHAPTER **24**

The Women in My Life

EVERY JEWISH WOMAN in South Florida wanted to take care of the three of us. There were also a few women of other faiths who became part of our life in the nine years that I lived in South Florida as a single dad. During that time I dated more than seventy women. Nine of these relationships lasted three months or longer. Almost any one of those nine could have led to marriage, but I wasn't ready financially or emotionally to make that commitment. If you are expecting to read the explicit and uncensored accounts of my numerous escapades during this time period, I am sorry to disappoint you. I will keep this G-rated, both for you and for my children and grandchildren who will also be reading this.

The X-rated version may be found in a future book written by "Anonymous".

If you are also wondering how I became so prolific in my dating, I offer up the following explanation:

I was a good-looking guy then, and whether I was with my kids or not, it seemed that there were always available women to date. Friends were constantly fixing me up. Est seminars were analogous to cruising the Burger King. Having my sons with me at a restaurant, the beach, the park, or the Discovery Center in Fort Lauderdale was like a chick magnet. Acting and creative writing classes at Nova University and Parent Effectiveness Training classes were great sources of potential dates. Music gigs were always fruitful, especially weddings and bar/bat mitzvahs. People I met through my work with the Arthritis Foundation had children or grandchildren they wanted me to meet. Local newspapers published stories on single parents with pictures of me with my kids, and these articles brought in numerous calls from a whole other contingent. In addition, at that time there was a place in Fort Lauderdale called The Singles Center and on Sunday nights for a one-dollar admission, a person could attend one of three or four consciousness-raising sessions. Eventually I ran one of those sessions. It literally became so onerous for me to date two or three women at once that there were times when I had to take a month or two off to rest.

Some people go through life never having one special love. I dated nine memorable women during my life in Florida, and I really do consider myself truly blessed for those experiences.

In various parts of this book, I mention a girlfriend by name, so for your understanding and clarification, I offer my infamous nine and a little explanation about each of them. I present them in chronological order, although a few of these women came in and out of my life during those years in Florida.

Maria

It was a Sunday morning at the beach in Fort Lauderdale. The boys and I were playing in the water when I noticed a radiant young woman doing what appeared to be a slow-motion ballet on the sand a little way up from where we were. Whenever Josh and Noah were with me, it seemed that it was easier for me to speak to strangers. That was the case this day. I approached her and asked her about the "routine" she was doing. It turns out that it was tai chi, and Maria was both a martial arts aficionado and a devotee of Bruce Lee. At the age of twenty-one, Maria was recently divorced with a two-year-old son and lived with her parents. It was never an issue with her that I was thirty-four at the time. She was the youngest girl I dated, except for a twenty-year-old I met at The Singles Center and who never made it to my top nine list. Maria was beautiful and slim with long dark hair and magnificent features. She possessed a gentle, loving demeanor and became my entrée to discovering myself through tai chi. Classes were held on Thursday nights in the park in Fort Lauderdale and were led by a short, frail, sixty-eight-year-old master who once took a six foot burly student to his knees with an almost imperceptible move.

There were seventeen of us in those hour-long classes. The collective concentration of the group and the intensity of the experience made it feel as if the air were electric. Josh and Noah always came with me and played in an area adjacent to the class.

Maria and I were very much in love, but I always knew that her age and her son were factors that precluded anything further from developing in our relationship. In addition to her passion for martial arts, Maria was a very talented artist. One day she came to our home and painted a contemporary mural on the largest wall in our family room.

Parting after six months was unbearably sad for both of us.

Lorie

I met her during the est training. Dark-haired, charming, and well proportioned, she was born in Detroit and was now living in South Florida on her own. Lorie worked for a publishing company, and our mutual appreciation for literature as well as going through those two weekends of est seminars together created a unique bond between us. I always felt that she seemed to be on a mission to get married. She came to the B'nai B'rith all-star softball game and watched me pitch for my team, Kadima.

We loved going to interesting places with my kids. On one memorable day, we went to the petting zoo, and I have pictures of her holding two baby tigers there. She was never as engaging as she was in that picture.

After three months we both knew that we weren't "the one" for each other.

We wished each other well when we realized that our relationship wasn't going anywhere beyond a friendship.

Linda

Sweet and dainty, she was divorced with two little girls who were each a year younger than Josh and Noah. She was just about five feet tall with jet-black, shoulder-length hair. Although she was Jewish, she resembled a China doll. Her father bought her a leather furniture store in Fort Lauderdale. The smell of fresh leather greeted you as you approached the front door of her home and became more embracing when you walked inside. A magnificent white baby grand piano was the focal point in the living room. The décor was the nicest I had ever seen up to that point in my life's experience. After visiting Linda's house for the first time and seeing a wall with built-ins, Noah later remarked to me, "What I liked was the way the radio and record player and TV were stuffed into the wall."

We were a couple for over four months. Our kids got along well until one day there was an incident in which either Josh or Noah inadvertently sprayed her kids with a can of fake snow. It was accidental but caused an irreconcilable upset.

Linda reentered my life years later and invited me over for dinner after I had broken-up with Jana (see below). Linda was a good cook and had set a beautiful, intimate table. Candles illuminated the room, and soft jazz played on the stereo. It was a scene taken from "Romantic Settings 101." The only thing that disrupted this magical setting was that, fifteen minutes into our conversation, I remembered what turned me off about her the first time around.

I left with a migraine.

Jane R.

(Not to be confused with Jane, whom I met years later and who became my wife. See Chapter 48)

One of the most sensual and intimate moments a single guy can have without being on a date is getting his teeth cleaned and having an attractive young female hovering over him, her face so close to his and her hands in his mouth. Jane was my dental hygienist and after two teeth cleanings three months apart and fantasizing about her, I asked her out. She was an adopted child with loving parents who lived somewhere in the Midwest. Her face was seductive with blemish-free skin. With a well proportioned, but somewhat chunky physique, she was a novel diversion from my usual sleek-bodied girlfriends. Jane was really pushing for a committed relationship. After the second month, as my thirty-sixth birthday approached, Jane showed up at my house in a red Corvette.

"I rented this for your birthday, and it's yours for your birthday week," she exclaimed.

What a wonderful surprise.

I felt badly when after three months I realized that I wasn't into her as much as I was into that car.

Barbara

She was one of the greeters at an est seminar. Very slim, dark-haired, and modelesque, she looked almost prudish. I later learned that her parents were ecstatic that she moved back home to Florida. It seems that the last three years she had lived in California with two guys you wouldn't want to meet in a dark alley.

Looking at this nice Jewish girl, who could have guessed?

It took me until the third week to start a conversation with her. After the seminar we went out for coffee. I told her, "I already have a girlfriend, but you can be number two if that works for you.

Hey, it's est, and the title of this seminar is "Be Here Now."

This scenario fit perfectly.

We dated a little over three months until that fateful day she said to me (very un-est-like), "I'm sorry, but I can no longer be number two. I want to be number one."

Unfortunately for her, she was not my number one.

After seeing Barbara the morning after a sleepover at our house and wearing my red, white, and blue bathrobe, Noah said to her, "Oh, you're wearing that bathrobe. They all wear that bathrobe."

Meryl

We had numerous band gigs at a catering hall in Tamarac, Florida. If someone wanted a "kosher" affair, the owners, Meryl's sister and brother-in-law, would bring in a rabbi to supervise the kitchen for the evening, and they doubled the price. Meryl worked in the office and managed the books. One Friday evening I arrived early to set up my drums and spotted Meryl walking from the kitchen back to the office. I looked up from the bandstand and said to her, "You must be the infamous sister I've heard so much about."

Meryl's sister had mentioned her to me, but I never acted on the recommendation. Meryl looked like her sister but was a younger, even more attractive version. OK, slim, dark hair—you know by now what I like. It was love at first sight, but she came with some really heavy baggage.

Meryl's husband had been killed in a car crash three years ago while she was pregnant with their son. She had been a recluse since then, focusing her whole life on her job and her son. Her mom lived with them in Meryl's house. We started dating, and Meryl turned out not to be the sweet, demure girl she appeared to be, but rather a wild animal just released from her cage. (Please see the forthcoming book by Anonymous to read the details.)

We lasted five months together, until one day she met a man who looked almost identical to her first husband and was financially able to support her and her son.

A few years later, Meryl catered the food at Josh's bar mitzvah at our house in Coral Springs. Susan and Jana (see below for both) were there also.

Jana

I saw her at my first acting class and knew immediately that I had to get to know her. Are you ready for this? A twenty-eight-year-old blonde, blue-eyed shiksa. Every Jewish boy's fantasy. She was pretty, smart, and funny. Her dad had been a bank executive and in mid-life decided he didn't want to do that anymore. He bought a farm in

Davie, Florida, and started a landscaping business, plant nursery, and antique shop, which her mom ran. Jana was a lawyer and had lived in Brazil for two years. She was interested in international law but still had not passed the Florida bar. When Jana smiled, the world lit up around her. We fell in love, and she lived with me for about two months. On her parents' farm was a grove of leechee fruit trees. It was magnificent and looked like a scene from a Chinese forest. The fruit ripens once a year, and they had to pick and ship the entire crop to a buyer in Canada in a week's time. My kids felt close to Jana and her family and the three of us helped them that week. I will never forget the taste of the most delicious fruit I have ever eaten and the powerful sense of family and teamwork required to complete that harvest. Jana was part of my comedy improv group, Full House, which consisted of three girls and two guys. All of us had roles in the movie _Caddyshack_ (see Chapters 32 and 33).

She was concerned about passing the Florida bar after having failed previously. I told her that I would give her an absolute guarantee that she would pass this time. For weeks I had been studying with her and coaching her. It was obvious to me that while she knew her material, Jana was lacking confidence. My ruse was to place seven polished stones in a small velvet sack and hand her a note with the bag of pebbles.

The note read, "My grandfather passed these stones down to me. In the Jewish religion, the number seven has mystical significance. These seven stones are sacred, and whoever possesses them is guaranteed that whatever they wish will come true. The only catch is that the holder of the stones must absolutely want the wish to come true. Any doubt at all will negate the result."

Jana thanked me profusely and kept the pouch of stones in her pocket during her test.

She passed.

In the end, no matter how much we were in love, a Jewish guy with two kids was not her picture of how her forever life would be. A few years later, she heard that I was moving north and asked to meet me for lunch. She was dressed as nicely as I had ever seen her, and her long, flowing blonde hair was also done for the "date." We reminisced about all of our times together.

She cried.

I didn't.

My sadness about our relationship had ended years before.

Susan

Parent-teacher night at my sons' school was always a great event. As I waited my turn to meet the teacher, it was always interesting for me to watch the degree that most parents were concerned about their children's grades and scholastic ability. I knew what kind of students my boys were. I read all their homework and tests, so I really did not want this meeting with their teachers to rehash that aspect of their schoolwork. What I wanted to know was how my sons participated in class, how they interacted with the teacher and with their peers, as well as the teacher's impression of them. Susan was Josh's ninth grade English teacher. I was unexpectedly surprised when I first met her that night. She was a few years younger than me, slim, short dark hair, and really, really cute. She loved Josh and his sense of humor—the first teacher to ever express those feelings. I asked what time she would be finished, and we agreed to meet then for coffee. That was the beginning of an extraordinary relationship. On our second date, she told me that she had a crush on me. She really had me with that admission. Susan was probably, next to my wife, Jane (see next chapter), the sweetest woman I have ever known. She wanted desperately to get married and have children of her own, but she wasn't annoying about it. Her entire demeanor brightened my world, and if there is one woman I regretted not marrying, it was Susan.

Eventually my inability to make a commitment crippled the relationship and the curtain closed when she met someone else.

Susan will always have a piece of my heart.

Robyn

I met her on a blind date through a friend's introduction and insistence. Her home was in an affluent area, and I parked in her driveway and rang the bell. She wasn't home. After fifteen minutes of waiting in my car, I was about to leave when I saw headlights behind me and watched her pull her Mercedes into her garage. She apologized for her lateness and invited me inside. My friend had told me that if you were in a crowd of a thousand people, you would be able to immediately spot Robyn—charming, tailored, and slender, with short dark hair and perfectly tanned skin. He was correct.

I, on the other hand, had a full beard at that time and was dressed in jeans, a sport shirt with rolled-up sleeves, and clogs on my feet. She asked if I wanted wine, and I proceeded to have my first-ever glass of Pouilly-Fuissé.

She was divorced and had two children, a son and daughter, who lived with her. Her kids were a year younger than Josh and Noah, so we had a lot in common.

Most of Robyn's friends believed she was somewhat of a prude, but after dating her a few weeks, I discovered quite the opposite (please read the details of those experiences in a future book by Anonymous). After two months Robyn, who liked a clean-shaven look on her man, suggested I shave my beard. After much contemplation on my part and continued urging on hers, I reluctantly agreed.

I was in my bathroom and shaved off the right half and then went into the living room where Noah was playing on the floor. "Noah, check this out," I said as I first showed him the still hirsute left side of my face and then turned my head to reveal my shaved right side. He was shocked since he has known me with a beard for as long as he can remember. I am not a practical joker and, in fact, actually despise practical jokes. Immediately I felt remorse and apologized to him. Like Noah, I too was disturbed and distressed at my appearance once I had completed the removal of all my facial hair.

"What the hell happened to my upper lip? It disappeared," I thought. It took me a week to get used to my new look. Robyn immediately liked it and was very proud of herself for encouraging me to do it.

In addition to being the instigator for my new face, Robyn bought me a gold bracelet and a man's pouch to carry my "stuff." She was the first one to ever do my nails and taught me how to tie my sweater around my shoulders.

Essentially Robyn remade me in her image.

I kind of liked the new menschy-appearing guy that I had become. We dated for over a year. Every holiday at her spectacular home was always a wonderful event and a reason for Josh, Noah, and me to be part of her wonderful family that also included her dad, stepmother, and aunts. Robyn was a terrific cook and attended to literally every detail of the meal and the occasion. We made each other happy and, for the first time in my life, I really enjoyed being taken care of. One day while walking on the beach with her and having a discussion about our relationship and where it was going, I suggested that we had three choices: we could break up, we could get married, or we could keep enjoying each other and let it be.

We chose door number three, and it lasted that way another few months.

Robyn remarried after that. It just wasn't to me.

I am a strong believer that there are people in your life you will always love.

I wish each of these women happiness.

They deserve it.

CHAPTER 25

The Neighbors' Kid

ONE OF OUR neighbors' kids, Brian, lives about five doors away. He is two years older than Josh and has been growing like a weed. Brian and his younger sister, Steffi, have been friends with my kids from almost the day we moved to Coral Springs. Today Brian came over with a large box. "I have something for Josh and Noah," Brian eagerly exclaims.

"They're in Noah's room," I reply. "Come on in."

Brian drags the box into our house, leaves it inside the front door, and runs into Noah's room. Seconds later Brian and my boys appear and tear open the box. In it are four large and really neat, shiny Tonka toy trucks. This past week Brian turned eleven.

"I am too old for these now, and I want Josh and Noah to have them," Brian announces and proudly smiles.

My sons are truly excited to receive this unexpected gift.

"Wow, thanks, Brian," they proclaim almost in unison.

It is now a little after noon, and I ask Brian, "Do you want to stay for lunch?"

"Sure, I'll call my mom and see if it's OK," he answers. His mom tells him it's fine and to just be home by 3:30 p.m. After eating the peanut butter and jelly sandwiches I make for the three of them, they go out back to play.

It is now close to 2:00 p.m., and I look out through our patio doors to the lawn beyond, and they are still playing with those trucks. In fact, they continue to play at our house until it's time for Brian to go home.

After he leaves, I can't stop thinking, "It's really strange that Brian is too old for those toys at his house but not at ours."

CHAPTER 26

Just Fix It!

NOAH'S REMARKABLE MEMORY is one of the things I admire about him. He relates details of incidents that happened two years ago. He can focus on the specifics with nothing clouding his recollections. Even more praiseworthy is that he also remembers what and how he was feeling at the time.

With that bit of realization, an exercise I love doing when I am alone is to reflect on a certain incident in my prior life and try to re-member my feelings at the time—feelings that I was not in touch with at the time and certainly was unable to express.

That is how I grew up, unaware and totally out of touch with my emotions that were, in effect, an unidentifiable and invisible master who controlled me.

There are daily annoyances that occur in my life today that evoke negative feelings and which I continually endure. Earlier in my life, I had zero thoughts that these irritations even existed. Now, at least, I am aware they are there, but in most cases I allow these curable miseries to continue.

They plague me.

They oppress me.

But I still tolerate them and don't do anything to remedy the annoyance.

A terrific example of this is located at the side of my house. The door leading from the laundry room to the driveway has swollen from years of rain. This makes closing that door rather difficult. In fact, the door has to be literally full-force slammed to close it. The slamming causes the entire house to shake. I cringe every time I hear that crashing door. If I am in a negative mood, the noise from closing the door enhances that feeling, like someone driving a spike between my eyes. This has persisted for a long time.

I kid you not. Talk about living in a stupefied fog!

It's now been quite some time since Lois moved out, and I just noticed how I am feeling at this very moment as the door is once again slammed. The thought occurs to me, "Schmuck, if it bothers you so much, fix it, you idiot."

Or in the words of that famous philosopher, Ben Stern, "Don't be stupid, you moron."

I grab a screwdriver, and it takes me exactly ninety seconds to adjust the plate opposite the lock on that doorframe.

Ninety seconds to eliminate the slamming.

Ninety seconds to be at peace.

Just fix it!

CHAPTER **27**

A Ride to the Mall

JOSH AND I are riding to Broward Mall. Noah is at Lois's apartment. The weather is perfect—low humidity, sixty-five degrees, and not a cloud in the sky. In a moment of wild abandonment, we decide not to have the air conditioner on in the car and open the windows.

"What's the big deal about that?" you may be thinking.

Well, the fact is we just never open the windows, not in our car and not in our house. I don't know why, but please believe me, we don't. With the windows open, the world outside welcomes us with new sounds and new smells. The fresh air reminds me of when I was a kid and that brief time my father lived with us. He had a Nash Rambler, and we would go for rides up the boulevard (Roosevelt Boulevard) in Philadelphia. I was four or five at the time and can still remember how happy I felt during those rides.

While enjoying the fragrances blowing through the car, Josh and I share the fact that we love the smell of fresh hay. That common ground leads him to tell me something that he had not shared previously. "Last summer, when Noah and I visited Poppy and Grandmom up north, we were at a farm, and I climbed up to the hay loft and jumped into a pile of hay below. It was real fun, and I didn't get hurt. While there we caught a rat, and I was holding it before it escaped."

"Josh, that story reminds me of my physiology laboratory in pharmacy school and injecting rats and mice for experiments. We had to hold mice by the tail and let them latch onto the cage with their front paws. Then we would grab them by the back of their necks, flip them over, and inject them in their abdomen.

"There was one guy in our class, Ed Sica, who was my lab partner. One day a mouse tried to bite him, and he flipped the mouse against the wall. The professor saw this, came over, and said, 'That's not how we treat animals here, Mr. Sica.' "

Josh asks me about the purpose of those experiments, and I attempt to answer so that he can understand. After hearing my explanation, Josh says that he wants to be a vet when he grows up and have a house full of animals.

We finally arrive at the mall and purchase the books and supplies that Josh needs for school. Our shopping trip is a success, but the best part of today is the ride to and from the mall.

Fresh air—it's a beautiful thing

(VI)
WHEN ALL ELSE FAILS, TELL THE TRUTH

CHAPTER **28**

About to Lose Our House

LATE IN JUNE 1979, the state of my financial affairs continues to deteriorate and is bordering on catastrophic. On some days when I insert my credit card into an ATM, I pray while I await my fate—whether cash will come out or whether the machine keeps my card because of overdue payments. My largest financial pressure is that I have been continually late on my monthly mortgage payments. Adding to this debt is the fact that I pledged a second mortgage on my house as collateral for a Small Business Administration (SBA) loan for my failing business. My life is a financial disaster.

This all culminates one day when I receive the following letter.

United States Department of Justice

_____

UNITED STATES ATTORNEY
Southern District of Florida
300 Ainsley Building
MIAMI, FLORIDA 33132

CERTIFIED MAIL
RETURN RECEIPT REQUESTED
TO ALL PARTIES LISTED BELOW:

Re: Lot 8, Block "J," Coral Springs Country Club Subdivision, according to the Plat thereof, as recorded in Plat Book 60, Page 43, of the Public Records of Broward County, FL.

The file of the mortgage on the above property has been referred to this office for foreclosure by the Small Business Administration. It is to your advantage to reinstate the mortgage, in view of the current economic situation and the time and expense of litigation.

Please contact the Small Business Administration immediately and make the necessary arrangements to reinstate this account. If we are not notified of a reinstatement within 30 days of this letter, we will have no alternative but to proceed with the foreclosure suit.

Very truly yours,
J.V. ESKENAZI
UNITED STATES ATTORNEY

By:
ANA T. BARNETT
ASSISTANT US ATTORNEY
Mr. Melvin H. Stein
Mrs. Lois Stein
Re: Health Care Services, Inc.

This notice brings me to my knees.
Faced with the abyss of financial catastrophe, the only recourse I have is to lay it all on the line.

CHAPTER **29**

Baring My Soul

WITH NOTHING LEFT to lose, I make my stand "at the Alamo," un-armed and in a weak fortress. All I have left is the courage I discovered a long time ago during a hot Philadelphia summer in 1951.

Armed with only the truth, I respond to the SBA with this letter.

Small Business Administration   July 12, 1979
2222 Ponce de Leon Blvd.
Coral Gables, FL 33314
Attn: Mr. Kennedy

Dear Mr. Kennedy,

Per our conversation, this letter will serve as my written proposal for my loan repayment. I have exhausted the possibilities at the present time of bank refinancing or taking out a new second mortgage with a mortgage company. My monthly payments would be prohibitive for me right now, and I intend to keep my word on a repayment schedule to the SBA. At present I can afford to begin paying you $200 monthly and will meet with you every four months to review my financial status, should I be able to increase my monthly payment or be in the position to make a lump sum payment.

For your consideration, I want to briefly restate my

financial history of the past five years. In 1974 my company, Health Care Services, Inc., which had obtained a $25,000 SBA loan, went out of business. This was attributable in large part to four of our wholesale business customers declaring bankruptcy. One particular account, Da-Wen Drug Stores, Inc., went out of business while owing Health Care Services in excess of $14,000. I called the SBA office and informed Mr. McNally of my plight, and I voluntarily turned over the assets of Health Care Services to the SBA. At about the same time, my wife, Lois, left me and my two sons, aged at that time five and seven. I had no job and no funds, and I was concurrently informed by the Internal Revenue Service that Health Care Services owed $4,500 in back taxes for which I was personally liable. Everything I had owned—savings, stocks, jewelry, stamp collection—was sold to get my two boys and me through that period. In 1975 I started working for National Convalescent Aids, Inc. and was given the responsibility of running the company at an annual salary of $25,000. This gave me the ability to continue first mortgage payments on my house, start paying back the IRS and live on a week-to-week basis paying my bills. My contacts with your office, Mr. Kennedy, have informed you of my past financial status.

At present my salary remains at $25,000 yearly. I have also attained the positions of consultant to GHI Medicare, and president of the Arthritis Foundation of Broward County. My consulting payments will augment my salary to help meet my commitment to you and the SBA.

I have paid back virtually all that I owe to Internal Revenue with the exception of $338 for which they are willing to wait until next year's tax return. A potentially additional source of income, which I have previously mentioned to you, is the book I have been writing about my experiences as a single parent. I have attached an excerpt for you to read.

Mr. Kennedy, I plead to you that all I have left as far as

material possessions is my house. I have an excellent arrangement where I live for school for my sons and for their care after school while I am at work. I have a good job, and I intend to pay you back in full—I am not asking for any discounts. What I am begging you for is to not take away our home and to accept my payment proposal for now. I hope you can ascertain from the information I have provided that I intend to meet my obligation to the Small Business Administration.

I anxiously await your reply.

Sincerely,

Melvin H. Stein

A week later I receive a letter from Mr. Kennedy informing me that he accepts my proposal. My "Hail Mary" pass is successful, and at least for the moment, our home is saved.

Facing me now is the realization that I now have to deliver on my proposal to pay the SBA two hundred dollars a month. I am eking out a living at this point and barely making ends meet financially week to week.

A serendipitous event happens a few days later that will allow me to fulfill that obligation.

(VII)
WITH A LITTLE BIT OF LUCK

CHAPTER **30**

Ludwig and Zildian to the Rescue

A FEW DAYS after receiving the reprieve letter from the SBA, while checking Josh and Noah's schoolwork, I find a flyer in each of their schoolbags announcing "Performing Parents for Music in Our School Week." The flyer requests that if you are a parent who has some musical skill, please sign up to participate in an assembly program at Westchester Elementary School. The program will be held in two weeks.

My sons both ask, "Dad, why don't you play your drums at our school?" At this point in our lives, my drums sit in the corner of our family room. Although I play at times for my own enjoyment, I have not played professionally since my days as a VIP.

"It has been over ten years since I've played in front of an audience," I reply.

"Come on, Dad," they persist relentlessly, urging me to participate.

Not wanting to let them down, I cave in and agree to do it. In my mind I also don't want to embarrass them in front of their friends. For the next ten days, I am committed to serious practicing and playing along with records.

In the process I start to realize that I had put a piece of me away in the closet for a long time.

Two weeks later on a Wednesday morning, I schlep my drums to their school. I am one of five parents who demonstrate their musical talents in front of several hundred Westchester Elementary School kids. I still cherish a file of thank-you notes from the kindergarten to fourth grade children who attended this assembly program. Many of the letters feature a hand-drawn picture of a bearded, long-haired guy playing a set of drums that have a large "VIPs" painted on the front of the bass drum.

Comments from a few of the older kids include:

Mr. Stein,
You did great on the drums.
I think the whole school loved your performance.
April Vara
Mrs. Schemel's fourth grade class

Dear Mr. Stein,
I think you are a great drummer. I want to be a drummer too.
I want to have my own rock and roll group.
Your friend,
Chris Banazek
Third grade

And my favorite:
Dear Mr. Stein,
I like the drums too.
What does the VIP stand for on the front of your drums?
How did you get that name?
I loved your performance. I am going to get the same kind of drums with the VIP on it."
Love,
Jason Branscome
Third grade

One of the other parents in the program, a thirty something guy named Charley, is a keyboard player and singer who comes over to me after the program and says, "I'm beginning to get back into the music business as a sideline and already have some jobs lined up. I need a drummer. Are you interested?"

I am still recovering from my anxiety performing in the assembly program for all those kids and hoping that my sons are proud of me when I blurt out without a second thought, "Absolutely!"

Just like my first career in music that paid for most of my college expenses, getting back into music now becomes my ticket to ride to cover my commitment to the SBA as well as providing additional money to get me back to overall financial health.

Trust me, this really is miraculous, especially the timing.

My first band job with Charley is that weekend, and it turns into a steady two to three gigs a week. Also, just like my first time around in music, I meet numerous musicians along the way. This time my journey ultimately leads me to another keyboard player and singer, Marty Lacks.

Unlike Charley, for whom music is a sideline to his ice cream truck business, music is Marty's only career, and eventually I become his steady drummer. This provides me with a guaranteed supplemental income and ultimately to the formation of a whole new business, Bruce Martin Music and Entertainment.

Marty started his music career as a one-man band – singing and playing keyboard along with an electronic rhythm box. Eventually he developed a music business that consisted of five or six piece combos up to big band jobs. With clients that include hotels, catering halls, and all of the major condo communities in South Florida, our jobs consist of dances, shows with singers and comedians, weddings, bar/ bat mitzvahs, parties, and special event gatherings.

Eventually we have fifteen bands under the banner of Bruce Martin Music and Entertainment, which is physically located next to my medical supply business. There are some nights that we're overbooked, and I am the bandleader for the Mel Stein Orchestra. Most of the time, I am the drummer for the first team that in addition to Marty and me consists of our regular sax, trumpet, guitar and bass players plus a female singer.

On one major job for a national convention in the ballroom of The Breakers in Palm Beach, we have a twenty-piece band. Marty has no charts (music) for the players. With the professionalism and quality of the players, he doesn't need any. That night I am in awe of the twenty musicians who improvise every song on the fly. After many of the sets, I am blown away and keep thinking to myself, "If we were recording this, that was a take!" Whatever the venue, audience or band composition, Marty magically pulls it off.

As you may have gleaned, I am an emotional guy. Weddings, in particular for me, are evocative of both deep happiness and sadness, regardless of who is getting married. One Saturday at The Breakers, we have just finished for the night. As we are packing up, one of my fellow band members, Mario the sax player, relates this story to me. During the wedding ceremony, he overhears one of the guests asking another guest, "Who is that crying over there?"

The reply is "I'm not quite sure."

"I don't think he's with the wedding party."

"You know, he looks familiar."

"I've seen him before at another affair."

"I think it's the drummer."

My emotionality will continue to be a part of me that I have great difficulty repressing. Years later in 1991, I am on a first-class business flight from Philadelphia to Los Angeles. The movie being shown is *The Father of the Bride*, starring Steve Martin and Diane Keaton. About thirty minutes into the flight, the stewardess hands out the menu, which lists either chicken or steak as the main course. With my earphones on and totally absorbed in the movie, I am enjoying the flight. My traumatic moment comes when the stewardess starts to make her rounds, asking for our main course choice. Seated in seat 3-A, I can see out of the corner of my eye what is happening and that, in a matter of seconds, it will be my turn to announce my selection. The problem I am experiencing at this moment is that I am so choked up by the movie—thinking about how I would be at my daughter's wedding—I can't speak.

With my earphones on, I pretend not to hear the stewardess until she is in my face motioning me to remove them.

It takes every fiber of my being to barely audibly utter my dinner choice while managing to restrain my heightened internal sentimentality manifested by the palpable sobbing welling-up in my chest and throat.

In a moment of sheer brilliance, even though I really want chicken, I choose steak for the simple reason that it is monosyllabic.

CHAPTER 31

Back in the Saddle

DURING THE TIME my Health Care Services business was going under, I read an article about the U-Haul company in the *Harvard Business Review*. It described U-Haul at that time as not owning one bolt in the trucks, trailers and other transportation devices they rented. Rather U-Haul created pools of leased equipment and passed the investment and equipment depreciation tax credits to the investors in the pools. Investors also received a fixed percentage of the revenue that the equipment pools generated.

In addition to the medical supply and orthopedic appliance parts of Health Care Services, leasing of durable medical equipment (DME) was the major source of revenue. The ongoing problem was the fact that it took at least five months to financially break even on a leased piece of DME. The more business I did, the more in the hole I became since I had to keep buying more equipment and was continually undercapitalized. My brilliant idea was to apply the U-Haul concept to DME.

I write a business plan and spend my last five thousand dollars on putting together a legal prospectus to sell the deal to investors. My lawyer, David Leibowitz, is a Hassidic Jew and someone whom I trust with my last dollar. In fact, I almost did hand him my last dollar. David does a great job on the legal offering document, and I soon start making my pitch to a list of targeted physicians and other affluent potential investors. No one says it's a bad idea, but it doesn't represent a significant enough opportunity for anyone to write a check. After two months of making unsuccessful sales calls, I go back to my lawyer and say, "David, I am just about out of cash. Is there anything we can do to change the 'deal' to make it more attractive?" This brilliant Yeshiva boy ruminates for a moment, looks at me, and replies, "I have a client, Pow-Mac, who might be interested. They own racehorses and have had a lot of success. They have cash and know a lot of wealthy people. Here's their number. Call them." The next day I call and discover that Pow-Mac is actually Pow-Mac Stables. But more importantly, Pow-Mac is Ed Powell and Bill MacMurray.

I walk into their office on the second floor of an office building they own. On one side of the large room, behind what seemed to me the largest desk I had ever seen, sits Powell. Ten feet across the room, behind a twin of Powell's desk, sits MacMurray. Leibowitz called them ahead of my visit and told them about the opportunity I created and the offering document. They love the concept.

They love it especially because—now here comes another miracle.

Are you ready for it?

A few years ago, Ed Powell was in the DME business, and Bill MacMurray was the past president of U-Haul.

No, really, I'm not kidding.

Can you believe that? I couldn't!

One month later, as Health Care Services is going out of business, we start National Convalescent Aids (NCA).

Pow-Mac and I are fifty/fifty partners.

For the next three years, I build the business through my professional relationships—the Arthritis Foundation; the MS Society; numerous home health agencies; physician contacts; as the DME, Orthopedic, and Prosthetic Appliance consultant to GHI Medicare; and through my Saturday morning radio show, "The Medicare Advisor," on WAVES radio in Fort Lauderdale. National Convalescent Aids is doing very nicely as a result of my efforts and utilizing the

U-Haul investor model.

Then one day Powell and MacMurray have a falling-out and split. Powell purchases MacMurray's share of NCA and moves into my offices. Once he takes up residence in an office he builds in the rear of the store, he basically sits there, reads the paper, and smokes cigars all day. I keep the business going strong until I can stand it no longer and make Powell an offer to buy him out of his ownership.

At the time I make that offer, I have no resources to back it up, but another serendipitous event occurs two weeks later.

The owner of one of the home health agencies, from which I am receiving frequent orders for home care equipment, approaches me. I had mentioned to one of his nurses how my situation at NCA had changed recently.

He says to me, "National Convalescent Aids' business is basically Mel Stein. I would like to expand my home health agency into home care equipment and supplies."

His closing question to me is "Mel Stein, are you interested?"

Later that week Powell rejects my offer to buy him out. I don't say anything, and the next day Mel Stein Medical is formed. My new partner and I lease a large store in Lauderhill, and my music partners lease the store next to it. A month later my new enterprise is in business and hits the street running.

Mel Stein Medical has the center store in a strip mall on University Drive in Lauderhill. Robyn, my girlfriend, does the decorating and color coordination—gray and navy-blue. In the front of the store is a large display of hospital beds, wheelchairs, and other medical equipment. My office and a fitting room for orthopedic appliances are beyond that and then the accounting area. Way in the back, there's a warehouse that houses oxygen tanks, commodes, and the like. The back door on the right side of the warehouse opens to the rehearsal studio for Bruce Martin Music and Entertainment, a video screening room, offices for Marty Lacks and my two other music partners, and a receptionist out front.

I am back on the horse and riding very tall.

CHAPTER **32**

Acting Class

THE INSTRUCTOR INTRODUCES himself as Sidney James, a handsome, blond-haired, and fit gentleman in his fifties with a booming voice and heavy Scottish brogue. There are sixteen students, ages twenty to eighty. The class is one of the personal enrichment evening courses given at Nova University in Fort Lauderdale, and the title of this particular eight-week session is "Acting and Improvisation." It sounded very cool when I enrolled, and I am looking forward to expanding my self-awareness and developing a possible new venue for my sense of humor. Little did I know then, but in addition to developing a great relationship with the instructor, in that class there would be four others with whom I eventually form a professional improvisation group, one of whom would also become my girlfriend.

Sidney's initial instruction consists of basic stage techniques, use of gestures, props, and emotion. No one in the group has professional experience, although one guy, a policeman, professes to have been an actor prior to his joining the Davie (Florida) police force. The group progresses quickly, and by the third week, we are doing improvisation exercises.

Setup scenes from the class become great material that I bring back home to Josh and Noah. My sons and I spend countless hours entertaining each other with made-up TV commercials, sports interviews, and breaking news stories.

About halfway through the class, five or six of us, at Sid's invitation, start going out after class to drink beer at a local bar in Davie, Florida. I don't know about now, but in the '70s Davie still had a lot of cowboys, and it seemed that all of them wound up at that same bar. While I never was a big drinker, Sidney is. He loves beer and Irish whiskey. As much as he enjoys pushing the envelope when he's sober, given a few beers and whiskey shots, he is off the wall.

To maximize the effect of our ongoing skits, which continue from the classroom to the bar, Sid has some of us sit on one side of the huge oval bar and the others on the opposite side. In between and all around us are the cowboys and their girlfriends. The place is unbelievably noisy with constant country music blaring from the jukebox.

Our diatribe usually begins with Sid yelling something across the bar like, "Hey, Mel, did the sheep come in yet?"

"I just got notice that they're arriving tomorrow," I scream back.

"That's great. I really liked the trussed ones they sent last time," he replies.

About this time I notice some of the cowboys looking at us with contempt and at least one looking really angry, like someone has just insulted his girlfriend. Impervious to fear, Sid relentlessly continues his outrageous questions.

To this day I believe that it was an act of God that no one attacked us during those hilarious exchanges.

The slender blonde with blue eyes caught my attention the first night of class. Jana would eventually become one of my significant girlfriends. Along with Jana and me, three other members of our class—Phyllis, Hermine, and Bud—decide to form our own comedy improvisation group, Full House. We perform at local comedy clubs and large condominium communities' clubhouses.

One of my favorite parts of our show was the Full House version of *The Dating Game*, in which we have senior participants play the game with our made-up questions for the bachelorettes or bachelors. Bud, dressed in a tuxedo, would ask questions like "Make a noise that will make me laugh"; "What do you think about living together?";

"Say something sexy to me"; "If we were stranded on a desert island, how would you entertain me?"; and "Finish this sentence : I can never get enough___."

Midway through our show, each one of us in the group performs a solo act. The three very talented girls sing or dance. Bud is an opera singer and performs a wonderful aria. For my part I sit on a stool in the middle of the stage with a singular light on me. You can hear a pin drop before I start talking about my sons, and then I recite "I Drove My Son to School." The audience loves this part of the show and being the emotional sot that I am, so do I.

And so it comes to pass that the entire Full House group appears in the movie *Caddyshack*.

If you are familiar with the movie, Phyllis actually has a starring role as Rodney Dangerfield's girlfriend, the girl with cascading blonde hair who doesn't utter one word throughout the entire movie. The other four of us are true extras, except for Jana, who also is a stunt double in the scene shot in Key Biscayne where Dangerfield crashes his boat into the dock. Bud appears on the steps of Bushwood Country Club, watching a guy puke into the convertible. Hermine is in the golf course crowd scenes. Jana and I are in various scenes, but if you want to see me clearly, go online to YouTube and search for *Caddyshack* trailers. Or plug this address into your browser: http://www.youtube.com/watch?v=cDllSnBgkRo

Pause the video at 0:33 of the trailer. It is the scene at night on the veranda of Bushwood Country Club where Chevy Chase is talking to Lacy Underall. When you pause the video, you'll see a guy with a beard (me) seated in the lower right-hand corner.

One piece of ultimate *Caddyshack* trivia is that I was the only guy with a beard in the whole movie. *Caddyshack* is filmed in 1980 at Rolling Hills Country Club in Fort Lauderdale, which at the time is the only course in southeast Florida that has no palm trees. A portion of the club is cordoned off from the shooting of the movie for regular club member dining. One night it's a wrap for the movie and a five-piece band is playing in the member's area.

You are probably unaware, as I was, that Chevy Chase plays great keyboard. He sits down at the organ, and I sit in on the drums. We play along with the sax, trumpet, and bass players of the house band. The set we perform turns out to be exceptional and remains for me one of the highlights of my music experience.

The question I have left unanswered for you until this point is "How did we get into this movie?"

I will tell you now that getting my entire improvisation group into *Caddyshack* had nothing to do with acting, improvisation, or anything even remotely related to performing.

It has everything to do with my business at that time, National Convalescent Aids.

CHAPTER 33

Caddyshack

I WALK BACK into my store after fitting a patient for a back brace at a local hospital, and my receptionist says to me, "There's a guy in your office waiting to see you."

When I enter my office, sitting there is a guy who looks like "Joe Hollywood" with graying temples, an ascot, and sunglasses. His first words when he sees me are "I understand you're the only person in South Florida who can help me."

I answer, "I'm really flattered, but before you even tell me why you're here, there are two people with appointments waiting for me who I have to see first."

He replies, "No problem. I'll call the set and tell them I'll be late."

Needless to say, now he definitely has piqued my curiosity, and he absolutely has my attention. I leave the office and zip through my other appointments.

Thirty minutes later he tells me his story.

His name is Eric Seelig and he is one of the top costume designers in Hollywood, known for his work in *The Deer Hunter, Mommie Dearest, The Godfather, Part II*, and numerous others. He was a kind, thoughtful, and very intelligent man, who passed away in 1995. With the deepest respect I have for him, I share this story with you.

A few months before, he was shooting a movie in Boston when he discovered blood in his urine. He was rushed back to a hospital near his home in California, where he was operated on for cancer and had his bladder removed.

Caddyshack is his first movie since his surgery, and he is now wearing a urostomy pouch, which is coming loose in the hot Florida sun. He called local nursing services to get immediate assistance. All of the home health agencies to which I have given in-service training on ostomy care recommended that he see me. After listening to his plight and observing his problem, I spend the next forty-five minutes setting up a new procedure for him and creating a binder on top to give him extra security.

When I am done, he is very pleased, and I say, "OK, I did you a favor. Now you can do me a favor."

"What's that?" he asks.

I then tell him about my interest in acting and about Full House, my improvisation group.

"Can you get us in the movie?"

"Meet me for dinner at 7:00 p.m. at Rolling Hills Country Club" is Eric's reply.

I do, and he introduces me to Harold Ramis, the director, and Jon Peters, the producer. Excitedly I call my friends, and the next day my group meets with the casting agent. We are all accepted and wind up working two weeks on the set at an "extra" pay rate of $37.50 per day. Phyllis and Jana have to join SAG (the Screen Actors Guild) for their roles and probably are still receiving residuals. For me the thrill of meeting and working with Chevy Chase, Rodney Dangerfield, and Ted Knight is one of the highlights of my life.

As an aside, all of the scenes with Bill Murray were shot in California, so I never met him.

Life takes us on many journeys.

Some are truly unexpected.

(VIII)
REALIZATIONS

CHAPTER **34**

Sunday Morning

WHENEVER I HAVE extraneous appointments or meetings scheduled on the weekends, I notice that I get upset. They interfere with my normal weekend routine, which is going to the beach or park on Saturday with my kids and on Sunday mornings playing softball for my B'nai B'rith team. Yesterday there was an est meeting at the home of my friend, Don, from 11:00 a.m. to 1:00 p.m. Today I am the em-cee at our B'nai B'rith Lodge new member installation brunch, and there is no softball game. I realized this past Wednesday that I could continue to feel crummy about what was going to occur this week-end, or I could just accept it and not ruin the next few days.

I decided that having to spend my time at an est meeting on Saturday and the formal brunch on Sunday was punishment enough, and there was no need for me to pay additional penance by being annoyed about it the rest of the week.

Unexpectedly, yesterday's meeting at Don's house turned out to be a terrific prelude to a great day.

First, I meet some really nice people who are not stereotypical est freakos. After they leave, Don, who is a movie reviewer for a local TV station, shows me some videos of interviews he did recently in Dallas with Jane Fonda and Jack Lemmon. Don and I became friends through our men's consciousness-raising group. He and I are really funny together, even though I have noticed sometimes that we are the only ones who know what's funny. Josh and Noah are playing outside with Don's kids and went with them to a neighbor's garage sale. Josh bought himself a Kodak instamatic camera for fifty cents, and Noah paid a dime for a first edition Spider Man comic book. It's 2:00 p.m. when Josh and Noah return to Don's house with their proud new purchases in hand.

"Hi, Dad, look what Noah and I bought," Josh proudly proclaims. "Where are we going now?" asks Noah. I compliment them on their new acquisitions, and then the three of us discuss the next lap of our Saturday journey.

They suggest one of their favorite places: the Discovery Center in Fort Lauderdale. The decision to go there is easy and unanimous, since I love that place too.

It is Easter weekend, and the Discovery Center has a holiday theme. Josh and Noah are coloring eggs, and I am watching a glass blower, sixty years in the profession, perform his skill. He and I chat for about twenty minutes while my sons are engaged in their egg coloring. He tells me about his wife's arthritis and her new hip implant and that, at seventy-two, the demands of his profession and caring for his wife are getting difficult. Although he just started training an apprentice, the young man doesn't want to earn only twenty-five dollars an hour while learning. I would have thought that people would be willing to work gratis for the privilege of watching and learning from this master. We shake hands good-bye, I take his card, and I tell him that I will bring my sons to visit him at his studio in Davie.

Josh and Noah come out with their colored eggs. They are both proud of their artistry, and we all agree that it's a tie regarding who has the "best" egg. The next hour is spent watching the bees and other insects in the Insectarium at the Discovery Center. Seeing the inside of a working beehive is mesmerizing, and the three of us stand there transfixed as we identify the workers, the drones, and the queen. While we watch I tell my sons about this elderly lady in my creative writing class who is writing a book about the lives of bees. Each week she reads the latest chapter in her love story, whose characters are all honeybees with human names. As we're standing there, I also mention that there is a guy in the same class who pointed to this same lady and said to me that he was amazed that she is also in his art class.

I said to this guy, "I can't believe this woman is eighty years old. She is also in my acting class!"

This leads to a whole discussion with my kids about how some people live life to the fullest and that happiness comes from within, from liking and respecting yourself. It is a great teaching moment, but what I do omit during the discussion with my sons is a most miraculous aspect of this wonderful lady that occurred in my acting class.

Our acting class had morphed into an improvisation class. One evening the setup scene is a person getting on a train late at night. She is the only one on the train. At the next stop, another person gets on and sits a few rows behind the other rider. What happens next and who speaks first is left up to those two people. The scene can last as long as it takes to deliver a punch line. With this frail, gray-haired, and modestly dressed elderly lady, it takes about three minutes. She is the initial rider who begins the scene by choosing a seat on the train and then taking a book from her bag. For the next minute, she becomes absorbed in her reading and doesn't look up when the train stops, and the second rider boards. This other rider is a tall, blond, and handsome young guy who is not taking this class for personal fulfillment and fun, but because he actually wants to be a professional actor. After a few seconds, he chooses a seat about three rows behind and across the aisle from the woman. He proceeds to close his eyes and feign nodding off. Nothing is said for the next minute. Body language indicates that each rider is being jostled by the movements of the train. Finally, a line is delivered by this tiny woman that puts the entire class, including our instructor, onto the floor.

She looks up from her book, turns around to the young fellow three rows back, and exclaims, "I saw you looking at my ass."

What a truly special lady, and now, Josh and Noah, you know the rest of the story.

It's around four o'clock when we leave the Discovery Center and enter the antique store next to it. I love wandering around places like this, and it seems that Josh and Noah enjoy it as well. Eventually Noah spends fifteen cents on a small gravy pitcher shaped like a cow, and Josh finds a clear bud vase for twenty-five cents. While ringing up the sale, the man at the counter gives each kid a free 1943 zinc penny. My kids have the amazing capacity to acquire freebies wherever we are—cookies, lollipops, cash, toys.

I don't think they look destitute, but maybe I am in the wrong profession, and we should become professional vagrants.

After returning home, showering, and changing, we go out to eat crabs at a local restaurant, one of our favorite dinners and a great respite from Pizza Hut, Burger King, and my famous casseroles. Afterward we all put on our jammies and jump into my bed to watch TV. Snuggled up with a son under each arm, I am in heaven.

My expectations for the day were the opposite of how it turned out. Yesterday was kind of like not wanting to go to an event and resenting being there after someone drags you kicking and screaming. Then you wind up having a great time.

You think about how much you didn't want to go and realize how big of a schmegeggie you can be.

I remember this terrific day whenever I have to go somewhere I don't want to be.

Although I may still be a jerk about it, at least I now have hope that it could turn out like that Saturday in 1979.

CHAPTER 35

Big Boys Don't Cry

SUPERMARKET SHOPPING IS something that I have worked into my schedule at a most unusual time. Albertson's in Coral Springs is open twenty-four hours, and it's 2:00 a.m. on a Saturday night after finishing a band job when I usually begin my week's grocery shopping. Although I am still wearing a tuxedo from my gig, I do remove my bowtie so I won't look completely weird at this hour.

There are always a handful of people in the store at that time, out to pick up a carton of milk, a pack of cigarettes, or a six-pack of beer. Never in all my years of shopping at this hour is anyone else doing "serious" shopping with a cart-full of groceries, but there is one very special singular occurrence that left me with a story worth sharing.

By the time I finish roaming the store, it is close to 2:30 a.m., and my cart is overflowing with food and household products. I get in the only cashier line at this hour, and I am behind two people. The first guy is just checking out with his beer and smokes. I am now behind a middle-aged lady, and I can't see her purchase until she plunks it on the rolling checkout counter.

The thoughts that invade my brain as I'm standing in line and looking at what is lying there are those of total disbelief.

"Can it be? No, what the heck would she be doing in the middle of the night with this? What would inspire her to leave her home, get in a car, and drive to Albertson's at 2:00 a.m. for this?"

I try not to burst out laughing from what I am seeing and thinking.

To control myself I bite a hole in my cheek.

There on the counter is a toilet bowl brush.

I could understand a plunger but a brush?

Did she have a nightmare that her toilet was dirty and someone would find out? Did she have insomnia, and the only activity she contemplated was cleaning the bowl?

Were her other choices rotating the tires on her car or repaving the driveway?

What could motivate her to want to clean her toilet in the middle of the night?

And if there were a rational explanation, what is the rest of this poor woman's life like?

I started to feel really sorry for her, and to this day the toilet brush lady remains for me one of the great, unsolved mysteries of all time.

In addition to my weekly supermarket schedule, there are rare occasions on which Josh, Noah, and I go shopping together. Whenever this happens, it becomes a fertile venue to have fun and for me to be a kid with them. There are opportunities down almost every aisle. Yesterday was an especially memorable trip.

Josh has just caught a terrific twenty-yard toilet paper pass in the cookie and cracker aisle for a touchdown. Not bad for a ten-year-old. Noah, two years his junior, is going long in pickles and condiments when he is unexpectedly tackled by a shopping cart.

Upon seeing the attempted catch and subsequent stop, an older man with his wife by his side remarks, "What a big boy. He didn't cry."

I continue down the aisle with my sons, complementing them on the scoring drive and rubbing Noah's bruised shoulder. After reflecting on what just happened, I'm sorry that I didn't stop the well-intentioned man to ask him, "What would have been so terrible, so unmasculine, so un-big-boyish if the kid had cried?"

Crying itself can make you feel better when you're really hurt.

I also know that sometimes crying can make you feel better even when there is no physical pain.

CHAPTER **36**

Righting an Injustice

"YOU GUYS WANT to go out for dinner?" I asked them when I picked up my kids from the babysitter after school today. It has been a difficult and busy day at work, and I am really tired. The last thing I feel like doing is going home and making dinner.

"Yeah, Dad" is the unanimous response.

When we get home, I decide I am actually too tired to go out again, but after my offer of a dinner out, I don't want to say that to my sons.

While I'm washing up, I hear them arguing over a toy. I fly out of the bathroom and tell them that because of their behavior, we aren't going to a restaurant. Josh looks at me and says, "If you don't want to go out, just say it," and runs into his room.

"That kid is so smart," I'm thinking. "He nailed this one."

I feel ashamed and upset with myself about the "punishment" I have imposed for not only such an insignificant incident but also one that requires no imposition on my part.

After several moments of "what do I do now?" racing around my head, I proceed to Josh's room. He's sitting on the floor, and I sit down next to him to explain what I had done and what I was feeling.

"I guess it's hard to be a kid sometimes. There seem to be a lot of injustices. It's hard for me to be a dad sometimes, too. I try to make the correct decisions, to give you the appropriate answers, and to do what's right, but sometimes it doesn't come out that way."

Josh and I discuss what happened, and I acknowledge that he was accurate. After I apologize for my erratic response, I give him a big hug and kiss his head.

The injustice I had inappropriately dealt to my sons has been corrected.

I realize that sometimes a parent is the policeman, the judge, and the jury. The judge can never let his emotions at that moment dictate his decision.

For me this experience is a lesson in restraint, in patience, in fairness, and most importantly for me, in keeping my word.

Dinner at Pizza Hut is especially good tonight.

CHAPTER **37**

Welcome Home, Dad

MY BUSINESS TAKES me on occasional trips, and I just returned from a two-day meeting in Washington, DC at a national health care conference. While I am away, Josh and Noah stay at Lois's apartment for the weekend. I'd asked Lois to bring them home around 3:00 p.m. today, which is about the time I expect to return.

What a wonderful surprise when I walk into the house and my kids are there. Lois dropped them off about fifteen minutes ago. It has become part of their responsibility to be by themselves. Although we are together most of the time, this has been happening more frequently now that I have band jobs and acting class. Because this is before cell phones and extensive wireless networks, I always leave them the phone number where I will be so they can call me if they need me. They have each stepped up their responsibility to take care of themselves now that they are ages eleven and nine.

After hugging and kissing them, I notice a sign that Noah had posted on the wall by the front door, and I realize how truly blessed I am.

It reads, "Welcome home, Dad!"

Sometimes I think I am the wealthiest man alive.

Noah will never realize how much his expression of love means to me.

Years later Noah will give me a birthday card that I still cherish.
The card reads:
"Happy Birthday, Dad. Everyone tells me that I am just like you.
And do you know what I tell them?
Thank you!"

CHAPTER **38**

Life Barometers

THERE IS ONE device that I have discovered is invaluable to refocus me on being introspective and, as a result, helps to extricate me from any cloud of negativity or depression. This tool is actually a practical and visible manifestation of how my life is going at any point in time. I share this with you in the hope that this will trigger your own personal barometer. Trust me, it works!

Individuals should have a "barometer" they can conveniently observe to give them immediate feedback on the status of their life at that moment. Just like a golf swing—easy to observe what imperfections are going on with others, but most difficult to see yourself—so it is with our own lives. Sometimes you're in a funk, and you don't even realize you're there, or if you do, you don't have the insight to question why or what is really going on. The first step is simply observing what's happening. If you get your life to the level of self-observation, you are now in control to do something about it. That's where a personal barometer is essential.

For me that life-measuring instrument is my houseplants.

Plants have always been a love of mine. They require pruning, feeding, watering, appropriate lighting, adequate containers or planting, and esthetically pleasing arranging. All of these are focused, albeit mindless, activities that require concentration and commitment while providing or demanding no mental stimulation.

Immediate gratification with no demands—what a great activity!

The houseplants at our Florida home occupy the covered patio that extends outside the sliding doors from our kitchen and family room. The floor of our kitchen is white brick, which is also the floor of the 12-foot by 30-foot patio beyond the glass doors that separate the kitchen from the outside. The white floor and the green lawn and shrubbery outside the patio provide a beautiful frame for the forty-two plants that reside there. Some are in pots on the floor, while others are hung with chains affixed to the wood beam rafters that form the underside of the patio roof.

There are various palms, crotons, schefflera, sea grapes, and other assorted tropical plants. Each is like an old friend and has its own story about how it was acquired, transplanted, and placed in its spot of honor. As beautiful and meaningful as each is, they are all subservient to my most prized specimen: a magnificent staghorn fern that hangs proudly in the center. Because of its large size and weight, the staghorn is planted in a fifteen-inch-wide ceramic pot and hung with four chains that go underneath the pot and attach to the large center wood beam beneath the roof of the patio. Since all of the plants are just beyond two sets of sliding doors, there is immediate and constant feedback about their state of health and "happiness."

It was years ago that I first noticed the correlation between my plants and my life. When life was good, so were my plants. Caring for them was a joy, which came easily when I was feeling good about everything else. Droopy, yellowing plants reflected lack of care and attention. There was a direct relationship between caring for my life and tending to my plants. The converse was blatant. If I hadn't been caring for my plants correctly, I wasn't tending to my life either. My plants were a constant reminder of what was happening in my life. My plants, my personal barometer, became a daily reminder to get back on track if I had gone astray. All of this became excruciatingly clear to me one fateful Wednesday in July 1980 during a period when many aspects of my life were not going well and a convergence of crises was about to occur.

Although my plants have been reflective of my lack of attention for several weeks, I have been so depressed and consumed by my problems that I really don't care. Financial anxiety, car problems, work conflicts, and issues with the kids have just about buried me. I can't get out of the funk I'm in. And then the final straw occurs.

Last night I broke up with my girlfriend, Jana.

On top of everything else, my heart is broken.

This morning I wake up enveloped by an even heavier cloud of despair. And yet, as despondent as I am, all of that horrific weight suddenly pales in comparison to what I see when I walk into the kitchen and glance outside.

I can't believe my eyes.

Lying on the white brick patio floor is my beloved staghorn fern. The ceramic vase, which crashed to the floor when the chains gave way sometime during the night, is scattered in thousands of shards across the patio.

It is like someone has smacked me on the head with a baseball bat.

My barometer is in the red zone!

Without a second thought, I go outside and begin cleaning up the glass and dirt. I repot the fern in a new container that I have stored in the garage. Then I drive to the hardware store and purchase heavier chain that will support the weight of the plant and container.

Restoring my fern is a critical step for me to regain control of my life. Later that day, after returning the staghorn to its position of honor, I feel both relieved and empowered.

At this critical moment in my life, I needed something to shake me out of my torpor. My plants rescued me and gave me the awareness to take a step back and regain control of my life.

Everyone needs a personal barometer.

My plants continue to serve as mine.

CHAPTER **39**

A Lesson on Being the Adult

SOMETIMES I BELIEVE that there is nothing I can teach my kids about being good people. I mean I can certainly teach them not to play with fire and not to jump off the roof, but I cannot teach them the insight or sensitivity they possess. They can see through my daily problems, my insecurities, and somehow, through it all, they clearly understand me.

They demonstrate their empathy and caring in totally different ways. Noah can sense when something is bothering me. He looks at my eyes as if he's studying me. He'll come over and put his arm around me or sit in my lap. He knows when I need his affection.

Josh, on the other hand, goes right for the jugular.

Last night it was about ten minutes before I had to leave for my acting class. Even though they have their own bathroom, Josh and Noah love to use the sunken tub in my bathroom. They like to fill it up and slide off the step into the water. I open the bathroom door to tell them to finish because I will be leaving soon. Water has overflowed onto the floor, and in my haste to have things in order before I leave, I get upset and yell at them. I follow my tirade by throwing their clothes at them in the shower.

"I want you out and the floor dried in five minutes," I scream.

Exactly five minutes later, I open the door and see that my demands have been met. The floor is perfectly dry even though they used every towel in my closet. All the wet items are piled into a neat

◀ 150

stack on the floor. Then I notice that their clothes are still lying in the shower. "Good job, but why didn't you pick up that stuff in the shower?" Josh looks at me with all the wisdom of the Delphic Oracle and asks, "Why did you throw them at us?"

Once again Josh gets me good. They were having fun in the shower and certainly didn't intentionally wet the floor. I could have just as easily told them to clean up the mess without losing it.

I am blessed to have kids who continually teach me how to be the adult.

CHAPTER **40**

Brothers

MY SONS ARE different in many ways that extend to how their rooms are decorated and arranged. Josh's room has bunk beds and is perfectly organized. He sleeps on the top bunk bed in his room and enjoys the ladder climb to his "perch." The sheets and covers on his bed are methodically arranged. Noah has a queen-sized waterbed on the floor of his room. There are usually clothes on the floor and an assemblage of toys, boxes, and other random articles spill out of his closet. Various pieces of his artwork adorn his walls. Noah enjoys "floating" somewhere in the middle of his bed, with the covers organized however they fall each night.

The three of us have just spent a terrific day in the park, celebrating Josh's twelfth birthday with a bunch of friends. It was a great day for a picnic, and all the kids and grown-ups enjoyed themselves. Everyone committed to bring an essential part of the meal to the celebration. My proud contribution was a six-foot-long hoagie and a chocolate and vanilla birthday cake adorned with an icing pictorial of Superman. The writing next to the caped crusader read, "Happy Birthday, Josh."

I enter Josh's room and climb the first few steps of the bunk bed ladder so I can reach him.

"Thanks, Dad, for a great birthday," Josh says sleepily.

I kiss him good night and go into Noah's room to do the same.

Noah is still awake and looks up at me as I bend down to give him his goodnight hug and kiss. In the next instant, I experience an unexpected "proud parent" moment. During the activities this afternoon, a strange kid came over and, for no apparent reason, shoved Noah. Seeing his brother on the ground, Josh ran over from the tree on which he was playing and punched the stranger who ran away. This incident received only brief discussion until now.

"Did you have fun today?" I ask.

"I did, Dad," Noah responds.

"Will you please gimme some juice? "No, wait. I think I should start drinking milk. Gimme milk so I can get big and strong like Josh and beat up people who hit me."

A bond between siblings that is formed by love, trust, and respect is one of the greatest gifts a parent can receive.

It is the hope of every parent.

Whether that bond will stand the test of time is not in a parent's control.

That's one of the reasons we pray a lot.

CHAPTER 41

Gallagher and Sheen and The Rat Pack

THE THREE OF us are a unique team bound together by much more than our genetics. Two places that we love visiting are Vizcaya, located in Key Biscayne, and the annual art fair in Coral Gables. The ambience of each of these is dominated by the beauty and uniqueness that surrounds any visitor. In the case of Vizcaya, it is the splendid architecture, the numerous fountains, and the exquisite gardens and flowers that connect it all. The Coral Gables Art Fair is a colorful event with hundreds of artists in booths, and the exceptional ethnic food and local music that form a superb backdrop to this great annual event. Both of these places create exceptional "Kodak moments," of which I have hundreds of memorable examples.

As we roam through the eclectic crowd at the art fair, we stop at booths of various artists and artisans who are especially appealing to us. One of these is an artist named Palnik. Paul Palnik is a Jewish American artist whose pen and ink cartoons are described in Wikipedia as "equal parts graphic design, drawing, poetry, and literature. Each Palnik cartoon can be likened to a one-page book dispensing wit, wisdom, and spiritual advice."

The one piece that especially attracts our interest, and the one we wind up purchasing, is a framed poster entitled "Blessings and Curses." It depicts numerous cartoon characters reciting things such as "May you get disgusted with yourself on a regular basis." Adjacent to that frame is one that reads, "May you understand what is important for you to understand."

There are over a hundred and fifty of these blessings and curses frames magnificently drawn and written on this piece of art. Placed in the middle of the poster is a blank space, which for an additional five dollars, Palnik fills in with a cartoon and a blessing right there on the spot as you wait. We buy the piece and opt for the fill-in frame. Our poster now has one frame that depicts the three of us and reads, "May Noah, Josh, and Mel always be together in love. May they become One." To this day that poster hangs proudly in my office.

Our family is one place where we can each be ourselves.

We each have our own personality as individuals and in relationship to each other.

We can laugh at ourselves and at each other.

We can get upset or angry, and it's still a safe place to be.

The fact is that we are a team—the three of us.

Kind of like some vaudeville act that had its moment in time—to be cherished forever.

CHAPTER 42

On Turning Forty

SEPTEMBER 27, 1983, 12:30am

Aging depresses me.

I don't feel adorable anymore.

More often now I think of myself as a man and less as a boy.

Somewhere along the way, I stopped noticing the daughters and started looking at the mothers.

I remember when that "boy" concept was first challenged, and the transition to an adult became a reality. It occurred the year after I graduated from college, and I went down to the Temple University bookstore to buy a sweatshirt.

The kid behind the counter said, "Can I help you, sir?"

Sir? I'm still a boy!

Before taking me to work with her, my mom brings me to Horn and Hardart for breakfast. We sit at the counter. She has a cup of coffee, which comes with a thick glass thimble of cream. I have a glass of milk and a glazed doughnut. Because my mom drinks it black, she gives me that tiny container of cream, which I happily slurp down. Twice a year we take two PTC trolleys to visit Aunt Kitty and Uncle Charley, my father's only relatives, other than Grandpop, that stay in contact with us. Uncle Charley is blind and earns a living selling newspapers and magazines at a newsstand. Their dimly-lit apartment reeks from the three cats that roam the place. I plead with my mom to never make me eat there. Thankfully, she respects my request. The positive part of these trips is the bundle of comic books Uncle Charley always gives me. My favorite is "Scrooge McDuck".

Every Saturday morning I take the subway downtown for my drum lesson. My teacher is Dave Levin, and his partner, Lenny Payton, writes jingles for commercials. Lenny shares with me his latest creation for car dealer Sunny Stein (no relation), who's known for his generous trade-in deals and who is always pictured with an orifice in his skull. It's to the tune of "My Funny Valentine," and it goes:

"My funny Sunny Stein
If you take this car of mine,
You've got a hole in the head."
Nice one, Lenny!

My mom is working late, and I walk from our apartment to Linton's on the 4900 block of North Broad Street. I sit at the counter and order a vegetable platter and a glass of milk. After finishing dinner I pay the $1.17 tab and leave a dime and three pennies as a tip. I'm ten years old.

Eight kids are playing "Spin the Bottle" at a junior high school party. It's my turn to see what fate has in store for me. The bottle points to a chubby, freckled blonde with a gentle, embracing smile. I kiss my first girlfriend, Gwendolyn Webb.

Just the other day I explore North Philadelphia on my bicycle. I pass my synogogue, Beth Judah, on Eleventh Street, and the memory of the most moving and magnificent voice I ever heard echoes in my head. Cantor Jehudah Mandel taught me my bar-mitzvah torah portion. Somehow I knew at the age of twelve that I was in the presence of greatness.

At my junior prom, two innocent teenagers sway on the dimly lit dance floor. I am slow dancing with Kathy McCracken to the music of "Theme From a Summer Place."

When I'm a senior at Plymouth Whitemarsh High School, I buy my first car, a used '55 gray and white Chevy Bel Air, from Mike Kardon Chevrolet in Cherry Hill, New Jersey. On the way home, riding on the Schuylkill expressway, it starts raining. When I turn on the wipers, they start scraping against the windshield because there are no rubber blades.

The other night The VIPs are on an enormous stage at the majestic Holy Cross Church in Springfield, Pennsylvania, just outside Philadelphia. On the floor beneath us are a few thousand dancing and screaming teenagers. We are wearing our "Beatle" suits, which is one of the three outfits we have. I actually like the look, but the other guys are sick of it. In addition, after wearing this outfit for the last two years, the Beatle suits are starting to look a little tired and showing wear. Little do I know that my fellow VIPs have a surprise in store for me and for the crowd. We're playing "Shout" and are somewhere in the middle of the song when Steve, our guitar player, sidles back to me and says, "Whatever happens, keep playing."

The music is excruciatingly loud when I scream back, "If you lay a hand on me, I'll kill you." Steve responds, "Don't worry, just keep playing." Well, I'm back there playing a loud, steady beat with my aluminum drumsticks and a golf glove on each hand when, one by one, each of the other four VIPs stops playing. Then, in an instant, they appear to be fighting and start ripping their unknown to me pre-slit Beatle suits off of each other. Underneath each is wearing long red underwear. The crowd loves it, screams, and applauds. I keep playing the heavy backbeat of "Shout" as Joey, Jerry, Steve, and Joel, now in their red pajamas, pick up their instruments. We finish the song, the set, and the night. For the rest of the evening, I remain in shock but still wearing, for the last time, my Beatle suit.

And now, all of a sudden, I'm turning forty.

Sir? Are you kidding me?

CHAPTER **43**

Yogi Berra

SUNDAY, MARCH 3, 1985

Here I am again at the beach in front of the Hilton in Fort Lauderdale. Noah is next to me, sitting on the sand and reading. This is a "déjà vu all over again" scene from ten years ago. My problems are more numerous today than ever, even though I have gained introspection and matured emotionally to at least my chronological age. Money issues continue to abound, and I still work week-to-week to get by. My hair continues to fall out, and I am growing less cute by the day. I'm dating two to three women at the same time and in continued infatuation with at least one of them. Josh is having problems with his grades and recently got arrested after he and a friend were caught smoking grass in school. I got the call and sped to the police station. When I arrived and saw Josh, frightened and alone, I hugged him.

"I'm sorry, Dad," Josh said barely audibly, tears streaming down his face.

The other kid's dad arrived. He saw his son, started screaming, and angrily slammed his kid against the wall.

After speaking to the police and signing some papers, Josh was released into my custody. The hearing would be in a week. On the way home, I told Josh that he would have to undergo whatever punishment was determined at the hearing. I also told him that I love him.

He was given a three-day suspension from school and a mandate to attend substance abuse classes.

In addition to this latest adventure with Josh, I still haven't filed my last two years' taxes. I have developed leukoderma, which causes nonpigmented areas on my hands and face. Josh starts driving by himself next month. Noah is thirteen and has not had a bar mitzvah.

The list seems endless, but one thing that has taken me a long time to learn is that life eventually works out.

Problems get resolved, opportunities occur, and miracles happen if you are open to them.

In spite of all the "tsuris," life is good and I am glad to be alive.

(IX)
BUSINESS AS UNUSUAL

CHAPTER **44**

Why Big Companies Fail

EARLY IN 1985 Humana, a large health-care organization that is looking to get into home care, approaches me and my partner in Mel Stein Medical to acquire our company. Humana's management believes that our business would be a logical and profitable extension for the several hospitals that Humana owns in South Florida.

During the courtship process, they fly us out to Humana's headquarters in Louisville, Kentucky. In addition to discovering that it's not pronounced "Louie Ville" but rather "Luhvull" (as if you had a mouthful of crap when enunciating the name of the place), management tells me that it is Humana's intention for home health care to become one of the largest divisions of the company. As I sit in Humana's huge marble conference room, I can't stop thinking that they really understand my brilliance and value, and I start envisioning a wonderful future for me as an executive at Humana.

It is now four years after Mel Stein Medical was formed.

After two months of due diligence, taking inventory, negotiating a price, and drawing up the agreements, we sell the business to Humana. Literally, as soon as we sign the papers, I am called into another room and quickly discover that my fate will not be quite exactly what I envisioned.

They will pay me the salary to which they have committed, but it is not Humana's intention to have me be an executive in the organization. Rather, I will become an employee of Humana in the role of a "detail man," calling on doctors to promote the business.

Oh, and there is one other thing.

In their large corporation's empirical wisdom, the first thing they will do is change the name of my business from Mel Stein Medical to "Home Care Partners."

For the past four years, this business has been all Mel Stein: my contacts, my reputation, and my personality.

In a nanosecond they suck the life out of me and out of the business. To say that I am dejected, despondent and depressed from these unexpected events would be a gross understatement.

As part of the purchase, I have a three-year earn-out and an employment agreement from Humana.

One month after the acquisition, I go back to my Humana management contacts and make an offer that will put me out of my misery. My proposal is that I will take ten percent less on the earn-out if they pay me a lump sum now. Also I will leave the company immediately, and both sides will be released from the employment agreement.

They agree.

Once I leave the business, it takes less than five months for them to turn all that I had built over the years into zilch. On the other hand, I have a pocketful of cash for the first time in my life.

Now what do I do?

CHAPTER **45**

A Miracle Encounter

WHEN YOU ENCOUNTER a miracle, you better be aware of what is happening and even better prepared to take advantage of the opportunity it presents.

October 1985

It's Saturday, and Josh and Noah are at Lois's tonight. I can honestly say that I do need some time alone. After considering my options, I decide to drive to Miami Beach and go to The Forge on Arthur Godfrey Road. The food is good. I can dine alone in the dimness without feeling self-conscious, and this place always has a good band that will keep me entertained for a few hours. As I am being seated at my table, I am totally unaware that a miracle is about to happen, and as a result, my life will forever be redirected.

In the next few seconds, I bump into a very old friend whom I haven't seen for at least ten years: Bob Allen. He worked for Leonard Abramson and me at Medical Equipment Unlimited. Bob was at least fifteen years my senior and, while a good sales guy, was very forgetful.

One of my most memorable Bob Allen stories occurred on a trip back from Baltimore where Bob and I were teaching an MEU training class.

We decide to stop at Walber's on the Delaware for a well-deserved, upscale dinner. It is now about 7:00 p.m., and the place is bustling. Bob is driving and parks his car at the outer edge of the crowded parking lot. We have pleasant conversation at dinner, and after I sign for the check, we make our way out of the restaurant for a long walk to the car. Once we arrive, Bob is ready to open the car but can't find his keys. A bit of panic ensues because it is now approaching 10:00 p.m. We are both tired, and we want to get home. After exploring the ground around the car for the lost keys, I notice in the darkness a glint of what appears to be the keys still in the car's ignition. This is way before you just clicked your key to lock/unlock the door. The locking mechanism has to be depressed manually, which we did when we got out of the car a few hours ago.

"Bob, go back into the restaurant and get a wire hanger," I request.

"Good idea," Bob responds and treks back.

While Bob is doing his thing, I spot a rusty old hanger lying about twenty yards from the car. I pick it up, wipe it off, and slip the wire between the window and the rubber after fashioning a hook on the end. After two minutes of trying, I pop the lock up.

"Yes!" I congratulate myself under my breath.

Jumping into Bob's now open car, I start the engine and pull the car up to the front of the restaurant. We had purchased two celebratory cigars after our meal, and I light one, slide over to the passenger seat, tune to some fine jazz on the radio, and put my feet up on the dashboard.

I wait patiently for the next ten minutes until Bob appears at the restaurant door, sweating and disheveled, with a wire hanger in hand. I will never forget Bob's expression when he sees me relaxing in the car.

Somewhere in that story is a perfect script for a MasterCard "priceless" commercial.

My other favorite Bob Allen story happens when Len and I first hired him at Medical Equipment Unlimited.

As part of Bob's compensation package, Len is able to get Bob a company car. Every Monday morning Bob and I meet with Len to review the business. Len is so proud of himself that he was able to get Bob a company car that at every Monday meeting he always asks, "How's the car, Bob?" This literally goes on for over two months with the same question from Len every week and the same answer from Bob, "Fine."

One Monday when Bob can take it no longer, he provides this magnificent reply after the "How's the car, Bob?" question from Len:

"Leonard, you always ask me how the car is, and to date it has been great. Let's make a deal that you won't ask me about the car anymore, and I will make a promise to you. In fact, I will swear to you on the lives of those I hold dearest that if there is ever any problem with the car, you will absolutely be the first person I call."

I love that story.

So there in the Forge is Bob Allen, appearing from nowhere. What were the odds that I would meet someone from my past here? After the requisite greetings and quick mutual-history-update conversation, Bob asks, "Have you spoken to Len recently?"

"Actually, Bob, I've been living in South Florida for the past thirteen years and have not. What's Len up to?"

Amazingly Bob pulls out his wallet and folded inside is an article about Leonard and US Healthcare.

I mean here's a guy I haven't seen in over a decade who is walking around with this article folded up in his wallet. The piece of paper looked like it had been tucked away in there for years, but he knew exactly where he had it squirreled away and pulled it right out.

After reading it I am thinking, "Holy shit, Len really did it."

"Why don't you give him a call?" Bob suggests.

"Thanks, Bob, I think I will. Great seeing you!"

Now really, what are the chances of this encounter ever occurring? The Vegas line on this actually happening would be staggering!

CHAPTER 46

A New Life

THE NEXT DAY I search out Len's contact information, and on Monday I make the call. Although it has been thirteen years with no contact, it's like no time has passed when Leonard answers the phone.

"Mel Stein," Len says energetically. "What's going on?"

"Hi, Len, I just sold my business to Humana, and I've been lying on the beach pondering the mysteries of life," I happily reply.

"What do you want to do now?" Len asks me.

"I want to be happy," I answer.

"Come up and we'll talk" was Len's invitation.

Twenty-one days later, it's Thanksgiving week. Josh, Noah, and I fly up north for my meeting with Leonard.

Len, now the CEO of US Healthcare, makes me an offer I can't refuse. Afterward I tell my sons the good news, and they seem really happy about the move, even though they will be living quite a distance from their mom. When we return home to Coral Springs, I put our house up for sale, and we make plans to move back to Pennsylvania.

It's the day after New Year's 1986, when my kids and I start our drive up north to a new home (a townhouse I had rented), to a new school for my boys, and to a new job for me with a great salary, but with no title and no job description.

Noah, now fifteen, and I drive in my car, a 1981 Datsun 280

ZX. In the backseat is a cage that houses Mittens, our cat. Following behind is seventeen-year-old Josh in his bright yellow 1975 Datsun B210. Next to Josh, in a cage much smaller that the one housing Mittens, is Snaky, Josh's boa constrictor. As night approaches and after a few stops for meals and bathroom breaks, we pull into a Days Inn somewhere in North Carolina.

"No Pets Allowed" a sign prominently states.

We enter the lobby, and I sign us in at the reception desk. Then we drive around back to where our room is located. The three of us try unsuccessfully to control our laughter as the great pet caper unfolds, and we covertly smuggle cat and snake into the room. It is now also after 11:00 p.m., and we are worn out from the long ride.

Sleep comes easily for the three of us with no time to contemplate the next phase of our life on which we are about to embark.

CHAPTER 47

Starting From Scratch

IT'S 10:00 P.M. and pitch-black outside when we find Jolly Road in Blue Bell, Pennsylvania and make it to our rental town home at Korman Suites. After the two-day drive north from Florida, we are all exhausted. I flip the lights on in the darkened house, and the first thing that strikes me is that the carpets aren't light gray as the leasing agent had promised but rather a very dark, disgusting brown. The moving truck delivered our household possessions the day before, and boxes fill the dining room from floor to ceiling. I am feeling kind of scared about the unknown that lies ahead and really depressed about the crappy carpet, but I manage to keep it together and remain strong for Josh and Noah.

The next few days are spent getting them enrolled in school, opening an account with the electric company, and getting a phone number and various other requisite household activities. It is also spent fulfilling my promise to my sons that when we moved to our new home, I would get them a puppy.

We go to a local breeder and pick out an adorable female black Lab, who will go nameless for the next two weeks before we officially decide what to call her. Like a multitude of serendipitous events in my life, a name for our pet flies in from left field.

I am sitting across from a young lady at US Healthcare who is explaining the workings of our member services department. While she rambles on, I became fixated on the nameplate staring at me from her desk. It reads "Gert Freas."

All I can think is, "That's it, what a great name."

I can't wait to tell Josh and Noah that evening.

From that day forward, our little puppy that grows into a frolicking, the-world-is-my-playground dog is "Gert."

Josh and Noah seem to adapt well to their new school, Wissahickon High. I start US Healthcare with no idea about my role in the company.

As God is my witness, this is exactly what happens the day I arrive: "I'm here, Len, and ready to get to work. What do you want me to do?"

"Go upstairs and run medical delivery" is Len's reply.

I move into my office with no idea of what medical delivery entails and, like most other things in my life, make it up as I go along. There are three physicians and twenty-five nurses for whom I am the administrative overseer. I start having discussions with each member of my team and begin to see the opportunities that abound. I see what I am doing as mining a field of gold nuggets. Every time I bend down and pick up a chunk of gold, I discover another vein underneath.

"This is really going to be a lot of fun," I think to myself.

A few days later, I have a meeting in Lehigh Valley with one of our key doctors there. He is upset that we have been late on our payments to his group. I promise him that I will look into it as soon as I get back to the office. He thanks me and says, "I expect a callback tomorrow."

"You have my word," I reply. We shake on it, and I leave.

The next day, after reviewing his file, I call and tell him that he is definitely owed the money he claims and promise him that in thirty days he will have a check to bring his group current. I then ask our head accounting guy to run the numbers and make sure that the doc has a check in thirty days. On my calendar I place a reminder three weeks out. The end of the third week, I call the accounting guy and ask him what day the check will be mailed, "because I promised this doc that by next week he will have the money we owe him."

The accounting guy tells me, "I'm really busy and haven't even started going through this account." This genius then says to me, "And you should never promise people things like this."

I'm feeling a lot like Rodney Dangerfield at this point. That's when I go into Len's office and tell him what has occurred. Len is one of the most honorable people on earth. His word means everything, and I know that recounting the numbers guy's comment about never making promises will get Len's attention.

"Len, I need a title in order to get some respect and to be able to get things done."

The next day Len gives me the title of vice president and increases my salary by ten thousand dollars.

The doc gets his check two days later.

One of my favorite US Healthcare stories happens after my first three months on the job. Len calls me down to his office, and when I arrive, he introduces me to Bill Epstein, a gracious and professional older guy who also is Len's family dentist. Bill comes to US Healthcare once a week to review mandible surgery claims covered under our health plan.

"Well, Bill," Len begins, "your dream is about to come true. We are going to start our own dental plan, and you will oversee it from a clinical and quality of care perspective, and, Mel, you will put the whole thing together and set it up." Len rambles on for a few minutes about a dental plan while I am screaming to myself in my head.

Finally I can stand it no longer, and I blurt out, "Len, let me ask you one question. What the hell do I know about a dental plan?"

I swear that what I relate to you next is exactly as it goes down.

Without missing a beat, Len stares directly at me, pauses for a second, and then delivers one of my all-time favorite Len lines:

"You have teeth, don't you?"

In three months we launch US DentalCare, which I name. It becomes the first HMO dental plan in the country.

That is just how things happened at US Healthcare— an unbelievable sense of family, an overarching entrepreneurial spirit, a pervasive no-bullshit policy, and a benevolent dictator, Len, who ruled it all.

Len would frequently roam the halls and walk into offices and not only ask people what they were doing at that moment, but also what were they doing that day to make money for the company.

In my eventual capacity as senior vice president, one of the national accounts I was most proud of acquiring was General Electric. It took over three years for me to close that deal. Len would constantly ask me about it. The day finally arrived when I walked into Len's office with the signed agreement from GE, and Len's comment was "That was yesterday, what are you doing today?"

I am blessed to have a Len Abramson in my life, someone who opened doors for me, who became the greatest mentor I could ever have, who treated me like a big brother, and who saw talents in me that I never recognized in myself.

While at US Healthcare, I started five businesses within the company, which all came from customers asking for help with some problem or opportunity. Len's office always has an open door for me where I can share my ideas with him. If he likes it, he says, "Go do it!" If he has any doubts, his response is "Create a business plan and come back." Any ideas that require a business plan are immediately discarded. They are even removed from my "Ideas Brilliant and Not So Brilliant" file.

I am never afraid to put my ass on the line for a concept in which I have a strong belief. There is one especially memorable example that occurs when I am senior VP of the company and had just returned from a trip to JC Penney in Plano, Texas. At that meeting the head of Penney's human resources asks me if US Healthcare can do anything to help manage her employee disability and workers' compensation programs.

The next day, when I get back to the office, I approach Len with my thoughts about starting a managed workers' comp business. He is so unimpressed that he doesn't even ask me to write a business plan for it. Knowing that I have a winning concept, I say to Len, "A national expert on disability and workers' comp will be in our area in two weeks. I met this guy at a conference, and he started a successful but fledgling workers' comp management firm in Tennessee." I then turn the tables and say to Len, "I will make you an offer you can't refuse."

This really gets Len's attention.

I propose, "Spend thirty minutes with this guy. If you think it's a waste of your time, no questions asked, don't give me a bonus this year."

Len smiles broadly, and we shake on the deal.

A few weeks later when the meeting finally occurs, Len doesn't spend thirty minutes. He spends almost two hours with the guy.

Workers Comp Advantage is created, and yes, I receive my bonus.

(X)
PHILLY BOY RETURNS

CHAPTER **48**

Jane

IT'S THE MIDDLE of January 1986. Josh and Noah are now settled into their new school and I at US Healthcare. At a family dinner, I reconnect with one of my cousins, Alison, who is five years my junior and someone I have not seen since the thirteen years I lived in South Florida. "Alison, you must have some cute single girlfriends," I ask. She eagerly replies, "Do you want a blonde, a brunette, or a redhead?" "You know, I have never dated a redhead. I'll go with that one," I answer without a second thought.

Alison scribbles the redhead's name and number on a scrap of paper and tells me to "have fun."

We talk for over an hour on the phone the next night when I call her. Jane turns out to be a southern belle with a detectable accent from growing up in Jacksonville, Florida. After being married for ten years, she has now been divorced for several years from a Jewish doctor. Her background is intriguing.

She lived with him in Mexico, where he went to medical school. Jane is a registered nurse who graduated at the top of her class from Thomas Jefferson University and is now a coordinator for worldwide clinical safety at SmithKline Beckman. She understands several languages and has traveled to France and England in her professional role at SKB.

It is immediately apparent that we have a lot in common—health care, Florida, failed relationships, and love of family.

Her parents live in Ponte Vedra Beach, just outside of Jacksonville, Florida, where, for the past fifty years, her dad, Dr. Joseph J. Lowenthal, has been a physician specializing in internal medicine and cardiology. Jane's mom, Freda, was the youngest of a large family. Freda's mother was a concert pianist who died when Freda was five years old. Freda's father was a ne'er-do-well who couldn't care for his eight children after his wife's death.

He sent the four eldest to live with relatives and placed the four youngest in a Jewish orphanage in New Orleans, where Freda was raised.

Freda and Joe were both loving and welcoming people who turned out to be unexpected blessings in my life—Joe as the father I never had and Freda as a second mother, especially after my mom passed away. At Joe's funeral years later, half of the city of Jacksonville attended. From the director of the Jacksonville Philharmonic Orchestra to the janitor of the synagogue, Joe was their physician. The policeman who accompanied the procession to the cemetery got off his motorcycle and wept at the gravesite. Joe had been his doctor. I learn that my father-in-law was instrumental in starting Shands Teaching Hospital, part of the University of Florida, in Jacksonville and that he routinely had scholarly discussions with the rabbi at his temple. I never realized the true greatness and the number of lives that Dr. Joseph J. Lowenthal touched. He was a man I loved and whom I was proud to call Dad. After Joe passed away, Freda moved from Jacksonville to New Orleans to be close to her son and his family. Ironically she now lives in a beautiful assisted living home less than a mile from the orphanage where she was raised. Up until recent years, Freda and I had spirited discussions about finance, world affairs, and sports. She was intelligent and articulate until Alzheimer's disease robbed her of that.

Jane has a fraternal twin, Janet, who still lives in Florida with her daughter, Annie, and a brother, Joe, an attorney who lives in New Orleans with his family—his wife, Dianne, and their children, Trey, Katherine, and Jack.

Jane and I meet a few days after our initial phone call. It is the middle of winter, and I appear at the door to her apartment in my buttoned-up coat and gloves. The door opens, and I am relieved that she is as adorable as she sounded on the phone: flowing red hair and petite, with a smile that immediately warms me from the cold outside. To this day she avows that at that moment she knew that I was "the one." It takes me a year and a half to realize that I'm not getting any younger and any cuter. It takes me a year and a half to realize that I am at another crossroads in my life and am faced with a choice. I can screw up this relationship as I have numerous others, or I may finally be ready to make the commitment. It doesn't take me a year and a half to know that I am in love with Jane, but it does take me that long to propose.

I get down on one knee in the middle of one of our favorite restaurants in South Philadelphia, Cent' Anni. She cries yes and can't wait to tell the world.

We're married on September 13, 1987, at Temple Rodeph Sholom in Philadelphia. The rabbi, a dynamic young guy from California, had never previously met Jane or me. A week before we're married, he interviews each of us to learn some facts that he can incorporate into his ceremonial blessings. He also proposes that he can wear one of three outfits for the wedding: his rabbinical robe, a nice suit, or his Lakers jacket. It's our choice. I really like the idea of the sporting motif, but Jane convinces me to opt for the traditional robe. During the ceremony, he wonderfully and magically intertwines Jane's and my comments from our singular meeting with him. It seems to everyone in attendance that he has known us from the time we were children. Len Abramson is my best man, and one hundred of our friends and family attend the ceremony followed by a reception at a center city restaurant. Jane and I are truly blessed and ready to begin our life together.

The few weeks before and after our wedding would prove to be the next turning point in both of our lives.

Events during that time set the stage for yet another miracle.

CHAPTER **49**

Our Honeymoon

FROM THE TIME I propose to the day of our wedding, there is a six-week window. We still joke that Jane didn't want to give me time to change by mind, but in actuality Josh has to leave for college the second week in September, and we want to get married before he goes away to Utah. In one of the greatest feats of tactical execution I have ever witnessed, Jane and her mom magnificently pull off every single detail of the wedding arrangements. Josh's leaving does pose a problem for our honeymoon, which Jane and I agree to postpone until after Josh is settled at school.

I am inundated at work, and a few weeks prior to the wedding, I ask Len for a suggestion where we could go on our honeymoon.

"We want a place that's not too far, has nice weather, and still feels special." Len thinks for a moment and suggests, "How about Bermuda? The flight is easy and only takes two hours. The weather is warm, and it's a great place for a honeymoon."

Jane loves the idea, jumps on it, and arranges the flight and accommodations at the Sonesta Beach Hotel on the west end of the island. We leave one week after I return from taking Josh to college.

The day we arrive for our honeymoon it is partly sunny, and we take some pictures outside on the sand. We don't know it then, but this will be the only chance we have for enjoying the waves and the beach in Bermuda.

The weather changes dramatically for the worst in a matter of hours. At this time in 1987, cell phones, hundreds of cable TV channels, and the "www" are not yet facts of our daily lives. Jane and I see the darkening clouds, but the only news on TV and radio is about the cricket matches, which seem to go on endlessly. There is no mention that Bermuda has not had a hurricane strike in the last thirty years and has not had destructive weather in the last forty years. With no warning and no news, the perfect storm hits on the second day of our honeymoon. Furniture is removed from all outside patios just before the first winds and torrential rain hit from Hurricane Emily. Windows are breaking in some areas of the hotel, ships in Bermuda's port smash against the docks, trees are blown down, and power is lost in the hotel and throughout the island.

For the next two days, we live in the hotel with generator-produced electricity. On the fourth day, with no relief in sight, we decide to get on one of the few buses to the now reopened airport and try to return to civilization. The ride to the airport, which is normally thirty minutes, takes over three hours because of the numerous stops we have to make for the men on the bus to get off and remove fallen trees and debris from the roadway.

When we finally arrive at the airport, we discover that departing planes are few and far between. There is no flight to Philadelphia but only to LaGuardia in New York. The other problem is that it is scheduled to leave twelve hours from now. Here we are, feeling like aliens in a third world country, sitting on the floor of the airport. We recognize some of the people from the hotel and introduce ourselves to what appears to be a friendly couple who are being approached by several other travelers. The couple turns out to be Mike Keenan, coach of the Philadelphia Flyers, and his then wife, Rita. They were vacationing at the Sonesta where we were staying.

I love sports and bleed Phillies' red and Eagles' green, but I have no interest in ice hockey. Other than hearing his name, I have no idea who Mike Keenan is and that last year he won a championship with a team full of young bucks. In spite of that, the four of us hit it off, and

Mike and I go foraging for whatever snacks and drinks we can find. In the meantime Jane and Rita get into a discussion about kids, and Jane is delighted to hear anything that Rita is sharing about her daughter. When Mike and I return with "the feast," we take a seat on the floor near the girls. You wouldn't think that a health-care guy and an ice hockey coach would have a lot in common. As we start chatting, the realization occurs that there are strong similarities between coaching a team of young guys who think they know everything and managing a sales force of similarly aged people with the same attitude as the hockey players.

It turns out that we get into some pretty heady discussions that last the long hours we spend on the airport floor. Twelve hours later our flight finally takes off. When we land Mike Keenan takes a cab to the game that the Flyers have with the Rangers in Madison Square Garden. I rent a car and drive my new wife and Rita back to Philly, where our cars are parked. It's 3:30 a.m. when we finally get home.

Little did we know that during the few days we were stuck in our hotel, our marriage would be unexpectedly blessed.

Prior to our getting married, Jane and I discussed the possibility of having a family of our own. We both agreed that it would make the most sense to start the process after a few years of marriage. Although Jane is undoubtedly the most nurturing person I know, being a mother is still not in her immediate plans. Having another kid is certainly not in mine.

But on our honeymoon with a hurricane outside, a lot of wine, and not much else to do but stay in our room, a miracle happens.

Almost nine months to the day later, June 18, 1988, our daughter, Alexandra, is born.

CHAPTER 50

Off to College

Josh

September 1987

I took my son to college this weekend confronting all of the hopes, dreams, and fears that come with that event. Josh was not the greatest of students in high school but was still accepted to several colleges from which we could choose. In spite of the fact that it would be twenty thousand Mormons and Josh the Jew, Utah State was the large campus opportunity that Josh selected.

This will be the first time since he was born that Josh and I are separated for more than a few weeks. The reality of this fact weighs unspoken on both of us as we begin the three-day weekend to prepare him for the school year ahead. We fly to a state where neither of us have ever been, drive on highways we never imagined we would be driving, see spectacular mountains unlike any we had ever seen, and experience the outpouring of friendliness from the people in Logan, Utah.

Our flight from Philadelphia to Salt Lake City is mixed with the memories we are leaving behind and the excitement of the adventure ahead. Once we arrive we gather our trunks and boxes from the baggage claim and pick up our van from the rental counter. I have already mapped out the two-hour drive north to school. The highways appear newly paved and are easy to navigate as they cut a path through the mountains that gleam spectacularly in the late afternoon sun. The colors of early autumn are the most vivid we have ever seen, and the inescapable changing of seasons all around us provides a poignant metaphor for what is about to occur. By the time we approach the town of Logan, the sun has gone down and the lights illuminate the cathedral there like a beacon in the night. Entering the campus, we are met by student guides who give us the final directions we need to get to the dorm. The pit in my stomach is beginning to build, but I am resolved to stay strong for Josh.

After finding the right building and going up to check out Josh's dorm room, some senior classmen help us carry the numerous pieces of luggage that we had brought with us on the plane. As Josh and I unpack, the newness and excitement of the moment occupy all of our thoughts and conversation. It's now approaching 6:00 p.m. here, which is actually 8:00 p.m. eastern time. We're more than really ready for dinner and jump into our rental car to find a small Italian restaurant just off campus. As we both sit there at dinner, finally taking a breather from the travel and unpacking of the day, I can see from the sadness on Josh's face that the uncertainty of it all is beginning to overwhelm him. The tears he has been trying to hold back finally come. Sitting across from him, trying to restrain my own emotion, I can't speak for fear of crying myself. Instead I take Josh's hand and hold it—something I haven't done since he was a little boy. Josh allows me that gesture here in the restaurant, something that would have been much too embarrassing at any other time. But for this brief moment, we confront each other's fear—his of being alone, mine of letting go.

We talk later that first night at the hotel. I am able to speak then, even though my voice cracks frequently as my feelings once again well up. It is one of those talks where I get to say a lot of things I have wanted to say for a long time but somehow never did. It's wonderful to reminisce about his growing up, our times together, sitting in the rain watching him play football, the pride I always felt in him, and his support of me. I tell him that when I went to school for parent-teacher meetings, the teachers always wanted to focus on scholastics, but I wanted to hear what Josh was like in class. He always made me proud. I remind Josh about the Palnik picture we purchased at the art fair in Coral Gables and the frame that reads, "May Noah, Josh, and Mel always be together in love. May they become One." Josh and I go to sleep that night knowing that everything will be all right.

Saturday is spent getting his dorm room in shape and running out to the local Kmart to get those items we have forgotten or couldn't bring with us on the plane. These include numerous toiletries, a small refrigerator, a fan, some shelves, and a few posters. We both decide, after everything is in order, that Josh's room is without question the most happening room on campus. We laugh a lot, have dinner, and go to a movie to help keep our minds off of the inevitable separation the next day.

Sunday morning finally comes, and at breakfast we handle all remaining business. I leave him with adequate finances. We make a checklist of things to follow up on, and after copying down his mailing address and phone number, I scribble a note at the bottom of his list of things to do: "Call Dad Monday night!"

After exploring the student center together, I take him to sign up for the freshman orientation he is about to begin. I then place my son of eighteen years in the hands of the people with whom I would entrust his care for this next adventure of his life. He walks me to my car, and we hug and kiss each other. Although Josh is bigger and stronger than me now, it is wonderful to hold him close, knowing that these moments would be rare from now on—a harsh reality after kissing him good night for the last eighteen years.

I took my son to college this weekend, and we both grew up a little.

Noah

August 1990

West Virginia University is a five and a half hour drive from our home in Blue Bell, Pennsylvania. It's a straight shot west on the Pennsylvania Turnpike and then south to Morgantown, West Virginia.

Noah and I visited West Virginia University a few months ago and were blown away by the area's magnificent rolling hills, the elevated monorail that connected main areas of the campus, and the impressive Mountaineer stadium. The scholastic opportunities, course selection, and the warmth of the people made it clear that it was a great fit for Noah. Once the decision was made, we started our preparations for life at college.

It takes numerous shopping expeditions to purchase all of the essentials that he will need for his freshman year. Shopping for clothes with Noah is always an adventure. From the time he was five years old, he had a very definitive sense of style and what he does and doesn't like. Initially I viewed this as his stubbornness. Later, when I reflect on this aspect of Noah, I consider that perhaps it is his expression of rebellion or some unresolved anger. But as I have gotten older, my impatience and frustration with the Noah shopping experiences of years past are now replaced with an appreciation for his individuality. In any event, after numerous trips to Nordstrom and Macy's, Noah's gear is finally assembled, and two weeks ago we packed and shipped four large duffel bags to WVU. More importantly, we both have adequate time to emotionally prepare for this day.

For this official first time going away to college, a direct flight from Philadelphia to Pittsburgh and then a short connector to Morgantown will be the best way. Riding down the Schuylkill Expressway to the airport, we speak about everything except Noah's leaving. When we finally arrive, there is over an hour's wait before his flight leaves. This is precious time to remind Noah about how proud I am to be his dad.

"West Virginia really isn't that far, and I'm glad that you will be close by." I manage to repress my choking sentiment as I continue. "You're almost a man now, and I have seen that you're gaining independence and confidence. But I suppose I will always feel like the dad who danced around the house with you on my shoulders while the Disney Light Parade music played through the speakers on our bookshelf. I will always feel like the dad who, years ago when you were only eight, you held one night when I was sad beyond belief. I'll never forget that night—it seemed that my whole world was crashing in on me. The Small Business Administration was threatening foreclosure on our home from a business loan I couldn't repay; I had just broken off a relationship with my girlfriend, Jana; and I had taken out my frustrations earlier in the evening by screaming at you and Josh. Later, when I collected myself, I went in to apologize. Josh was already asleep, so I kissed him good night and came into your room. You were lying there on your huge waterbed and staring at the ceiling. I lay down next to you and could barely get the apology out when I started crying uncontrollably. All the pain I had inside—every fiber of it—poured out. You didn't try to solve my problems or tell me that it would be all right. You just allowed me to be there. And you hugged me for five minutes straight without saying anything. Imagine, the eight-year-old comforting his dad. It was the tightest and most secure hug I had ever felt. You changed my life that night and got me back on track.

"And you will always be the son who would crawl under my arm whenever I sat on the sofa. You will always be the son who was never embarrassed to be kissed by his dad in front of other people. You will always be the son who was years ahead of his time when you comforted a little girl in kindergarten whose parents had just separated."

Noah and I sit there in the airport, quiet for a few moments, with tears in our hearts of what we have left behind and with joyful expectations of what would be.

"This will be your first birthday ever that I won't be with you, and it will be a year of new experiences for each of us. Whatever happens and wherever you are, I want you to know that I will always be with you." It is finally time for Noah to board the flight that will take him to his new life away from home. We hug and kiss, and then I watch him board the plane on his rite of passage into adulthood.

I realize that regardless of how our lives change, he will still always be my baby—my little boy who a long time ago, when my world had buried me in self-doubt, rescued me and gave me the strength to continue.

CHAPTER **51**

Alexandra

JANE'S ENTIRE PREGNANCY is nothing short of joyous. She beams the whole time and along the way develops an intense fondness for baked potatoes and red sauce on anything.

It is 4:30 a.m. on a Saturday morning when she wakes me and says, "I'm having steady pains. Ooooh! I think this might be 'the time'."

I jump up and dress quickly while my normally type-A, bouncing-off-the-wall, energizer bunny wife goes into the bathroom and casually brushes her hair and puts on her makeup.

"Let's go," I urge.

Jane continues to take her time as I stand there waiting and holding her overnight bag. She had called her doctor who informed her that, because this is her first pregnancy, it might be a false alarm.

But the pains don't abate. Rather they increase in intensity and frequency, and thirty minutes later we're in the car racing down the Schuylkill Expressway in the early morning darkness to Pennsylvania Hospital in Philadelphia. When we arrive I park on the sidewalk in front of the main doors and seat my wife, now in active labor, into a wheelchair. After a quick trip up the elevator, a nurse greets us and takes it from there. I run downstairs to park the car, and by the time I return, I am told that the baby is already starting to come out.

After quickly donning a blue surgical scrub suit, I enter the delivery room where, indeed, the birthing process is underway. It happens so fast that there is no time for any anesthetic, and Jane is fantastic throughout the delivery. The pride I have for my wife at that moment is incalculable.

I have my camera out and snap a picture of the wall clock. It is June 18, 1988, and at 7:02 a.m. Alexandra is born.

When I hold my daughter for the first time, I look into her beautiful blue eyes and tearfully announce to her, "Welcome to the world."

We take her home the next day, which is a Sunday.

It is also Father's Day, and I have been given the best gift I could ever imagine.

CHAPTER **52**

My First Mercedes

IN NOVEMBER 1989, my prized Datsun 280 ZX was really starting to fail with 165,000 miles on it. It was time for a new car, and I decided that I wanted a Mercedes. While sitting at lunch one day with Len Abramson, I mention this to him. He asks me, "Why don't you get a Lexus?" I remind him of our first life together after Medical Equipment Unlimited was acquired by Spectro Industries.

"Len, you wanted a Cadillac, and nothing else would do. You were so proud of that huge dark blue car when you drove it. Well, I want a Mercedes, not a Lexus." He smiles and nods that he understands.

That weekend, Jane and I drive to the Mercedes dealer in Doyelstown, Pennsylvania. When we get out of my Datsun, I realize that this may have been my last trip in it. This car and I have been through a lot together.

I recall years ago arriving at the Datsun dealer in Florida. The 280ZX sitting out front in the lot immediately caught my eye. It was love at first sight. I remember saying to the salesman, "I have one prerequisite before we go any further."

"What's that?" he asked tentatively.

"I have to see if my drums will fit."

The car has a metallic dark gray exterior and a two-toned, dark and light gray leather interior. The "T-top" glass roof is removable manually, which makes it an almost convertible. It's a two-door, so the T-tops have to be removed to be able to access the entire backseat as well as the trunk. My drum gear includes a rectangular fiberboard case for the snare drum; chrome stands and seat; a large, double tom-tom fiberboard case; a zippered, canvas bass drum sack, a canvas cymbal and accessory bag; hi-hat cymbals and stand; and a folding, wheeled hand truck to carry this assemblage into the place where I'm performing.

The first step of this defining test is to remove the T-tops and gently place them on the ground.

Then like a physician performing microsurgery, I methodically place each component into every millimeter of available space. Fifteen minutes later, after experimenting with various configurations, the operation is complete. As soon as I replace the T-tops, I announce to the now relieved and happy sales guy, "I'll take it."

Over the next months and years, I will repeat this identical process hundreds of times. With practice I have been able to refine the procedure and reduce the loading/unloading time to less than five minutes. The most delicate part is the removal and replacement of the glass T-tops, which, because of my exacting technique, remain unscathed. The singular blemish on this whole process is the inevitable jerk who always seems to appear whether we're performing at a large condo clubhouse, The Breakers, or The Doral. Like a spectator in the stands watching the gladiator perform, he will stand there outside and watch me as I systematically remove the drums from my car. His face and body may change with the venue, but inevitably it's a similar, predictable old fart who will utter these words: "I bet you wished you would have listened to your mother when she told you to play the violin." Except for a brief smile as I continue about my business, I never acknowledge or respond to this remark. My smile is not really a response to this schlepper's attempt at wit but rather a reflection of what I am thinking, which is, "Hey, that's really original. I bet you think you're the only one who has ever said something so brilliant."

As Jane and I walk toward the Mercedes lot to look at the new cars, I glance wistfully at my Datsun and think, "Good-bye, old friend."

A few minutes later, we see a white 300E with red interior and fifteen hundred miles on it. After a test drive and the token requisite but brief negotiation, we buy it. We complete the paperwork, transfer the license plate, and I say good-bye to my trusty sports car. We then strap baby Alexandra into her car seat in the back and proudly drive home in our new car. This is on Saturday.

In the next two weeks, my new car causes an interruption of a business meeting and will be at the center of a very memorable experience with Noah.

On Monday I have a meeting with AT&T in of all the places I would least want to drive my new Mercedes, Newark, New Jersey. I choose a parking lot that looks the safest and then drive in. After giving the attendant five bucks to keep his eye on my car, I ask him to direct me to the correct building, and he gives me explicit instructions. Once I arrive at the AT&T office, I will tell you in total candor that even though we are talking business, for me the first fifteen minutes of the meeting is about the safety of my new car. Finally I get off it and start focusing on the discussion at hand. Unfortunately, my concentration on business is short-lived, when it is interrupted by a disconcerting knock at the door.

The four of us in the room look up toward the new entrant.

"Does anyone in here have a white Mercedes?" asks the secretary at the door.

"Oh shit," I'm thinking as my heart drops.

I envision the worst, raise my hand, and reply, "I do," to the young lady. She explains, "There's a parking lot guy downstairs, and you forgot to leave him your key. You're blocking the whole lot."

I quickly peel the key off of my key ring and give it to her.

"Thank you, and tell him I'm sorry," I respond thankfully, hoping that everyone else doesn't hear my heart pounding in my chest.

This anecdote sets the stage for a dramatic incident with Noah that happens exactly one week later when my son comes home for Thanksgiving weekend—his first trip back since starting college at West Virginia University.

After a wonderful four-day family weekend, on Monday Noah and I awake early to get the 7:10 a.m. Greyhound bus back to Morgantown. Noah has to be at school for classes this afternoon, and I have to be at work by 8:00 a.m. The timing of the bus is perfect. We leave the house at 6:30 a.m. It takes us twenty-five minutes to arrive at the bus terminal lot in King of Prussia, Pennsylvania.

The only bus sitting there displays "Los Angeles" on the front. We grab Noah's duffel bag and go inside the Greyhound building to buy his ticket. The bus to LA leaves at 7:10, but there is still no bus to Morgantown in the lot.

At 7:15 a.m. I ask the clerk, "Where is the bus to Morgantown?"

He answers, "That would be the bus to Los Angeles that left five minutes ago."

The Stein brain trust doesn't know that LA is the final destination for that singular bus going west, and of course, there is no listing of every stop the bus will make. "What route does the bus take?" I scream to the clerk as I grab Noah's bag.

"West on the turnpike," he yells back.

It is about 7:20 a.m. when Noah and I get back into the car. Resolute that Noah gets on that bus, I gun the car out of the Greyhound lot and onto the turnpike ramp about a mile away.

The bus has a ten-minute lead on us, and the race is on.

This is the first opportunity for me to see how fast my new car can go. The speedometer moves quickly to 120 miles per hour. Noah sits quietly as I focus on the road, mindless of any speed limit signs or patrol cars, which we fortunately don't encounter as we speed along. Today is a brisk, crystal clear November day. The fall colors magnify the spectacular view along this section of roadway. It's a shame we can't enjoy the scenery with the onus of catching that bus weighing on us. Finally Noah asks the obvious question, which hasn't occurred to me as I am myopically centered on driving as fast as I can.

"Dad, what do we do when we catch the bus?"

"I have no idea, Noah, but we'll figure it out when we get there,"

I blurt back.

We are now sixteen minutes into the race, and I am really impressed with the smoothness of the ride. It doesn't seem like we're going that fast. Finally I see something resembling a bus about a quarter mile ahead on a straight stretch of the road. As we get a little closer, I see the Greyhound emblem, and that's when the answer to Noah's question comes to me as clear as the sky above is today.

I start flashing my lights. "Roll down your window, and start waving your ticket," I yell over to my son. Noah follows my orders, and this goes on for about thirty seconds behind the bus—my flashing the car lights and his waving his ticket out the window. Mercifully and thankfully, the bus pulls over to the side of the road, and we pull behind. I lean over and kiss Noah good-bye. He grabs his duffel, jumps out, and enters the open door of the bus.

Later that day I call to see if he's all right and ask him what happened when he got on the bus. He tells me, "The driver took my ticket and acted like nothing unusual just happened. The only vacant seat on the bus was next to a nun who looked at me and smiled when I sat."

Although we are Jewish, I still take that as a sign from God, an indication that if you really want to achieve something, put your head down and go for it. Go for it and believe in your ability to accomplish it, in spite of any uncertainty or adversity, even when you're kicking yourself for being a dumb ass.

My new Mercedes, what a great car!

CHAPTER 53

Competition, Gambling, and Integrity

WHEN ALEXANDRA IS a year and a half old, we join Meadowlands Country Club in Blue Bell, Pennsylvania. The Sunday after my application is approved and I have paid my initiation fee, Jane, Alexandra, and I go to the club for our first Sunday dinner there. Alexandra is dressed in a beautiful pink and white outfit and is wearing her requisite headband. She looks like the perfect little girl, except she is climbing all over me like a monkey. Jane is a little embarrassed, but I am cool with it. As we sit on a sofa in the lobby, waiting for Josh and Noah to join us for dinner, I hear a voice next to me say, "Don't I know you?" I turn and look up to see who is speaking. Standing next to the sofa is an enormous frame of a man whom I immediately recognize. It's John Keane, the club manager at Meadowlands.

"John, you made a profession out of it" are the first words out of my mouth. Years before at Green Valley Country Club, I actually trained John to be a busboy. He still looks like that cute pudgy kid I remember—just a little bigger and a lot older.

At the age of forty-five, I revisit the game of golf after a hiatus of about twenty-eight years. To this day I still get a kick every time I see my name on the brass plate of my Meadowlands' golf locker. That pride comes from remembering my days working as a kid at Green Valley and before that growing up in North Philadelphia.

There are a few times I have been invited to play at Merion Golf

Club, one of the country's top one hundred courses. The number of Jewish members at Merion is somewhere between none and five. Adjacent to the first tee is a lovely outdoor patio where you can eat, drink, and watch the golfers tee off. Beer is served in a wonderful white ceramic tankard, and although I am not a big beer drinker, having one at Merion has become a tradition for me whenever I have the good fortune of playing there.

Drinking that beer at Merion and seeing my name on my locker at Meadowlands evoke very similar feelings: "Not bad for a Philly boy; not bad for a pharmacist!"

I have always loved sports. Growing up I play baseball, football, and basketball. Although I pitch and play third base on the junior varsity baseball team at Plymouth Whitemarsh High, I have to quit after my sophomore year because I need to work and save money for college. My football and basketball experiences are in pickup leagues and less formal than being on the baseball team in high school and the softball team when I lived in Florida.

Actually the one sport I really excel in is badminton. At Temple University I take badminton as an elective gym course. My badminton instructor recognizes my agility and my wrist and arm strength, and encourages me to pursue the sport. After a year of college competition, I represent Temple in the Delaware Valley Badminton Championships. In the semifinal match, I play the former badminton champion of Norway, Sven Nielsen, who defeats me in the best of three sets. A *Philadelphia Inquirer* newspaper clipping from that event is a prized memento of my badminton career.

When I start playing golf again after an almost thirty-year hiatus, it occurs to me that there is one aspect of the game that I can do as well as the pros: putting. I commit to becoming an excellent putter. I read everything I can find about putting and, like my awareness training, utilize the pieces that best fit me. By combining my golf studies with a lot of practice, I become one of the best putters at the club. Over the years I win the putting championship three times. The other aspect of the game that also attracts me is wagering. Some members of Meadowlands think that I am an inveterate gambler. The fact is that I dislike casinos, cards, and racetracks, but I do enjoy betting on golf and backgammon, two activities over which I believe I am mostly in control. Soon after we join the club and I first start golfing, I go out on the course late in the afternoons and play alone, because I don't want to embarrass myself. After a few months, I start to meet guys with similar abilities and we start playing together. It takes about two years before I become "one of the guys" and begin playing and wagering for whatever my golfing partners agree.

Golf has become my passion, and in addition to my extremely competitive nature, golf is as close an analogy to life as almost anything I can relate. Play a round of golf with someone and you know his character. You understand his risk tolerance, sense of humor, sensitivity, and courage or lack thereof. Most importantly you keenly know his integrity. Golf is a gentleman's game and as such is a game of rules to which players are expected to adhere. In the last few years, I have become more vocal with others about adhering to the rules as well as to keeping their commitments about games that they set up in advance. This has taken me to a point where I am no longer the most popular guy out there because I am so outspoken. Even though I will never forget what you did and will probably hold it against you forever, I will still play golf with you.

In a forthcoming book by Anonymous II, I will describe all the incidents of transgression in explicit detail and provide a list of the jerks and a-holes who committed them.

Jane asks me, "Why do you play golf with people you don't like?"

"Guys are different than women in that regard," I reply.

As I get older, I realize that there are no people I actually hate.

There are a few that I truly dislike.

There are many for whom I have no respect.

My greatest satisfaction is to go out on the golf course and kick their ass.

CHAPTER **54**

My Hero

ALEXANDRA, PETITE WITH blonde hair and blue eyes, is truly a blessing for not only Jane and me but also for my sons. Because of the age differences, instead of having two brothers, for Alexandra it was more like having three fathers. Josh and Noah treat her not as a frail little girl but rather as one of the guys. She loves every moment with them.

As she grows she develops Jane's southern sweetness and learns wonderful organization and study habit skills from her mommy. From me she absorbs my sense of humor and creativity. From both of us, she personifies compassion and integrity. Those traits are especially demonstrated for all to see on a particular Friday in the spring of Alexandra's fifth grade school year.

Field Day is an annual event at Germantown Academy for the lower school. Every class is divided into red and blue teams, and the athletic competitions are intense. Although Alexandra is the youngest and most petite kid in her class, the four-hundred-meter race (once around the huge, paved oval surrounding the football field) is her main event. There are eight girls in the race, and one of them appears to have legs longer than Alexandra's height. Jane and I, seated with the other parents close to the finish line, start screaming and cheering as soon as the race begins. The girl with the long legs is clearly at an advantage, but little Alexandra has the stamina and determination to make this a real race. In the final hundred meters, Alexandra, now in second place, actually starts to gain on Long Legs. I am screaming so hard I begin to lose my voice. It's now the last fifty meters and clearly anybody's race. Jane is in a cheering frenzy as Alexandra strides to the finish line as fast as her spindly legs can go.

That's when it happens—a true illustration of the quote from an unknown author, "Adversity doesn't develop character, it reveals it."

Suddenly and unexpectedly the girl in third place running almost alongside Alexandra slips and falls. Long Legs continues her surge to the finish line.

Jane is screaming at the top of her lungs, "Come on, Alexandra." I stop cheering and begin to well up with pride at what I am watching. My daughter stops in her tracks. Her humanity overrides her competitive instinct as she turns to help the fallen girl next to her.

Alexandra doesn't win the race that day, but her instincts and compassion make her my hero. Our pride in Alexandra will continue to grow as the years pass.

About eight years later, an event occurs that will help reestablish all of our priorities.

CHAPTER 55

What's Really Important

SEPTEMBER 11, 2006

It takes three days to move Alexandra into her dorm room in the Quad at the University of Pennsylvania, but the events since then are the most memorable.

For the past week, Alexandra has complained about a terrible headache that seems to be focused on the right side of her head. Last Friday we had her go to the student health center, where she was seen by the attending physician and given three medications for her headache. After a weekend of no relief, Jane and I go down to Penn yesterday afternoon to take Alexandra to a 5:30 p.m. appointment at the student health center after her last class. She is seen in fifteen minutes to determine or rule out the unthinkable possible diagnoses that the doctor has discussed. We are immediately escorted across the street to the emergency room at the University of Pennsylvania Hospital with a recommendation for an urgent CT scan.

It takes over three hours of waiting to make it into the actual emergency room from the waiting room. Even though Alexandra has been given the highest priority to be seen, her status is usurped by several ambulances, which arrive with heart attack and shooting victims who take precedence. We sit there in the waiting room in the midst of people with hacking coughs, patients doubled up in pain, and others throwing up in bags, which are thankfully provided. There are the anticipated drunks and cases of broken arms and legs. On the periphery of this three-ring circus of human misery, a few people argue in the corner as a nurse walks out and asks if there is a family member in the waiting room for someone who just died in the emergency room. A policeman stands watch at the door to make sure only patients and their families are given the privilege of entering the inner sanctum of the ER beyond the waiting room. In the middle of all this, the waiting room houses a really huge fish tank that, ironically, contains only two fish—a microcosm of the loneliness and suffering that exists in the room outside the tank.

Jane, Alexandra, and I position ourselves on two seats with a table extension that faces a small-screened TV hung on the wall. Old "Friends" episodes run continuously and provide some comic relief to this surreal setting that is so unfamiliar to the three of us. It is now approaching 7:00 p.m., and although Jane and I have no appetite, Alexandra is hungry since she hasn't eaten dinner. I spend the next half hour making several trips to the closest food, which is outside across the street. It happens to be a Chinese food cart.

My first excursion brings wonton soup, and after slurping it down, Alexandra is still hungry. I go out again and bring back chicken with vegetables and wild rice. Now thirsty, Alexandra wants a water and Jane, a Diet Coke, which are available in the soda machine near the waiting room. In my nervousness I don't put enough cash into the machine, and after nothing comes out, I believe that it's empty. I then make my third trip to the Chinese food cart and retrieve the water and soda. After the successful beverage run to my family is complete, I try to stay positive and maintain my composure while the uncertainty of what is going on inside Alexandra's head is tearing at me. It is now past the two-hour mark since we first entered the waiting room. Alexandra stays in good humor by reading her psychology textbook and discussing some of her revelations after only her second class. While sitting there I learn from Alexandra that the reason Freud had his patients lie on a couch looking away from him was that he couldn't bear to be spoken to directly for eight hours a day. Jane remains occupied by helping Alexandra organize her notebooks. I find myself pacing a lot, doing considerable praying for our daughter to be well, and staring at those two pitiful fish. The sign on the entrance to the ER reads, "Patients are seen in the order of their severity. The ER does not operate on a first come-first serve basis." The grammarian in me wonders in the midst of my anxiety if it should read, "first come, first served."

I pace, pray, hold back my overwhelming fear, and manage to maintain my composure when I speak to Jane and Alexandra. Mercifully, on the verge of not being able to take the waiting and uncertainty any longer, a nurse appears at the ER entrance and calls out, "Alexandria Stein." We enter the inner sanctum, and I tell the nurse, "it's AlexanDRA." She apologizes as she escorts us back to a gurney in the hallway outside the corridors of rooms filled with the troubled, the sick, and the poor. After another twenty minutes, which seems like an extra kick in the ass after the waiting room experience, a nurse comes over and indicates that an ER doc will see her shortly, but in the meantime, she says, "Are you able to give us a urine specimen?" Alexandra hasn't peed all night, so that request is almost a relief. Jane, a former RN, asks if a "clean catch" is required. Jane's attention to detail and to doing things correctly, even at this moment of high anxiety, is something that I have come to respect and admire. Jane assists Alexandra to the bathroom across the hall, and they return a few minutes later with specimen in hand. While we wait for the attending doc, the jar of urine, perched near Alexandra on the gurney, provides welcome comedic diversion as Jane almost twice knocks it over the edge. The next person to approach us is a young male medical student who says he has four questions to ask Alexandra in private and that it will take about thirty seconds.

In our worry, irritation of this intrusion, and our high anxiety, Jane and I step away. The kid is correct; it takes less than a minute, and he's done. Alexandra is quick to reveal the content of the inquisition. Has she been beaten, abused, or in any way harmed by her parents? Then, at last, the resident ER physician comes over to review Alexandra's history and perform the first physical of the long evening.

The doctor is a gentle and concerned resident who notices during her exam that Alexandra's right pupil is larger than the left. Jane jumps on this observation and adds that she knows every inch of Alexandra's body and noticed that same asymmetry outside in the waiting room. My heart starts pounding as this additional bit of "evidence" is added to the story. The doctor then tells us that the attending ER doc, who is also her "boss," would be in to review the case as well as an attending neurologist, Dr. Kranick. After fifteen or so minutes, the attending ER physician appears.

Dressed in sweatshirt and jeans, he has just signed in for his shift and hasn't had time to change. Requesting the same information dump that we have given previously, he appears to be in his late twenties and has a professional, pleasant, and calming demeanor. While assimilating the events leading up to now, he explains every-thing that has been done to this point and what was yet to happen to find out what is going on with Alexandra. As he talks and discusses the spectrum of what the problem might be, I listen intently but start shaking uncontrollably in fear of what I am hearing.

Most parents never want to be out of control, but at this moment I feel that I am totally incapable of doing anything to help. Pretending to be strong is all that's left of my ability to do something constructive. I am seated in a chair to the side of the gurney and, because of my positioning, hope that my trembling will go unnoticed by the others.

"To rule out a brain aneurysm, clot, or tumor, a CT brain scan will be performed. The resident ER doc as well as the attending radiologist read it. A neurologist will examine Alexandra, and those findings will then be added to the equation. After that the resident ER physician will be back to discuss all of the options and subsequent potential courses of action." But first the attending ER doc needs to talk to Alexandra without her mom and dad there. Jane and I walk down the hallway, trying to avoid looking at a disheveled patient puking in a basin and an elderly woman screeching in pain. Once the doc-tor gives us the "all clear" to return, he departs to see an incoming trauma patient. Alexandra reveals his private question to her: Was she pregnant, drinking or doing drugs?

The room outside of which we have been parked has been va-cated and cleaned during the resident's exam in the hallway, and the next step is for Alexandra to occupy the room and, per the doctor's orders, be hooked up to an IV through which she can be hydrated and receive two milligrams of added morphine. The mention of the IV and morphine brings the first tears of the evening from Alexandra. Jane and I look at each other with sorrow in our eyes and pain in our hearts but miraculously stay calm as we hug our daughter and assure her that it is the right thing to do. The charge nurse— a large, offi-cious, by-the-book lady—comes in to insert the IV and also to draw four tubes of blood required for lab tests. Blood pressure and heart rate are normal. At last some bit of good news. The nurse then asks the same questions that had been asked during both doctors' exams. In the midst of all this, the urine specimen, which was the first request from us once we had been admitted inside the ER, is now sitting on a table in the room.

That jar of pee has taken on a life of its own.

When we point it out to the nurse, she replies, "Don't worry, we'll get it. Someone will be in shortly to take her for the CT scan." It is approaching 3:00 a.m. when the orderly enters to wheel Alexandra's bed to radiology. I walk with them to the CT room and wait outside while the brief procedure is performed. Alexandra, now hooked up to the IV, is in reasonable spirits as she is wheeled back to her room. The morphine has taken a bit of the edge off her pain—down to a five-six from a seven-eight. Once back in the room, Jane and I hug and kiss her and give her whatever reassurance we can summon. I return to the hallway for another round of pacing, and while there, I see a young woman physician whom I hadn't noticed before enter the ER corridor. She wears glasses and has a small leather pouch slung over her right shoulder. "You look like the neurologist," I state. She con-curs. After directing her to Alexandra's room, she introduces herself to us, and the next round of the same questions begins. Feeling like the Ancient Mariner telling the same story again for the umpteenth time, we anxiously await the actual exam to begin. From her bag the doctor removes the test equipment to study reflexes and her ophthalmoscope to see what is going on in the back of our daughter's eyes. She agrees with the asymmetry of Alexandra's pupils but explains that it is not uncommon, even assigning it some medical term with which neither Jane nor I are familiar. Her conclusion, pending results of the CT scan, is that everything at this point appears normal. Although we are all exhausted at this point, the neurologist's findings provide some respite.

At last my trembling stops, even though I am unsure about what will happen next. Jane is noticeably relieved, and Alexandra is now asking for a drink of juice. We had been told by Nurse Ratchett "no food or fluids" with no explanation why. When we mention the nurse's orders to the resident physician, he indicates that there is no reason for that, and he will have juice brought into the room. A few minutes later, a kinder and friendlier male nurse enters the room with three apple juices in plastic cups and places them on the table. Alexandra reaches for one and asks me why I am smiling.

I say, "Be careful which one you take" because the still uncollected urine specimen is sitting on the table near the juice. We all laugh—a welcome release from the tension, which envelopes us.

For the next half hour, we try to get some sleep, Jane and I on chairs and Alexandra in bed hooked to the IV.

Sleep comes to no one, and at 5:00 a.m. the resident finally reappears. He is now dressed in hospital blues and has reviewed the neurologist's report as well as her read of the brain scan. The resident then repeats some of the same tests that the neurologist performed—neurological function tests and an eye exam.

He has Alexandra get out of bed and walk with her eyes closed to make certain that her balance is in order. His conclusion is that everything appears very normal and indicates that most physicians want to do more and that most patients want more—more at this point being an MRI and a spinal tap. If it were he and his family, he would take a more conservative route and try a drug specific for migraine. Jane and

I are reassured by his pragmatic and experienced advice, and agree to take Alexandra home and get his prescription filled immediately. We thank him, get Alexandra unhooked from the IV and dressed, note that the urine specimen is still there, and are given his discharge note and prescription. The time is 5:30 a.m. when we finally leave the emergency room at the hospital of the University of Pennsylvania. Jane and I are prepared to take Alexandra back home with us, but she has a different agenda.

She insists on going back to her dorm because she doesn't want to miss a 9:30 a.m. meeting with her advisor. Her explanation is that it will be more stressful for her to reschedule this than to go ahead as planned. We go outside in the early morning chill to the parking lot across the street, get into our car, and then drive two blocks where I park on the sidewalk in front of the entrance to the quad at Penn. I kiss and hug Alexandra as she gets out of the car, and Jane walks her down the path through the entrance gate. Still unsure about what will happen next, my only recourse is to look upward and pray for her health.

It's amazing how in a nanosecond we can be redirected to what is truly important: a renewed appreciation for the meaning of life, of health, of the value of family, and of the closeness and support that brings.

In that moment we realize the irrelevance of everything else.

CHAPTER 56

Growing Up

It seemed like my father's breath
always smelled of alcohol and cigarettes.
That same smell permeated our apartment—
The dank odor of an old bar
permanently etched in my memory,
bringing me back to my childhood in a nanosecond.

Sometimes I cowered in the corner
watching my father slam my mother against the wall.
Five years old and already deciding
that I would never express my anger.

Long after my father had gone,
waiting for my mother to get home from work
and crying uncontrollably when she was late.
Carrying my fears and anxieties alone, silently,
wanting to never worry or disappoint her.

Somewhere during the journey,
learning to be strong and take care of everyone
became who I am.

A crossing from child to adult that happens imperceptibly
like the gradual graying of hair.

Still a little boy inside,
I get a lump in my throat at a television commercial that is a reminder
of the past.
Anticipating that I might be really emotional when I watch my daughter graduate from the University of Pennsylvania.
Being all right with that.

At last, growing up.

CHAPTER 57

Reflections

THIS IS NOT the end but rather an ongoing story for me and for you. It's the learning from past experience that will enhance what lies ahead.

Some of what follows may sound a little "preachy". This is certainly not my intention and if you take it that way I apologize in advance. With that said, here are some of my reflections that I hope may make a difference in your journey:

A Parent's Role

Once my kids were no longer toddlers, and I wasn't there all the time, I learned that at some point they will be making choices in life for themselves.

I can't force-feed them only nutritionally correct foods nor eliminate less desirable intake.

I can't choose their friends or demand that they study (unless I were Tiger Mom).

I can't solve all their problems or always be there to rescue them when life presents them with difficulty.

At some point I will not be there to wipe their tears and care for their wounds and illnesses.

My singular job as a parent, and one I can control, is to have my children grow up feeling good about themselves.

With Josh and Noah, I regret that I learned this too late, but they are hopefully getting there as adults.

With Alexandra, I think Jane and I got it right.

Savor the Moments

Cherish every possible moment you have with your kids.

You turn around, and one day they are gone.

Josh and Noah never went to overnight camp, both because of my finances at the time and my horrible childhood experiences as a two-week camper at two charity camps.

At a Golden Slipper Camp in 1950, my counselor made us clean the floor with our tongues. The counselors were entertained by having the kids fight each other. Each night there were "boxing" matches in a fashioned ring. In my first and only fight, I was introduced as "Murderous Melvin." In pure survival mode, I had to beat up one of my friends. It was an experience so out of my character that at the age of seven, I agonized over what I had done for the rest of my miserable stay at that camp. I never told my mom out of fear of upsetting her.

At Camp Hofnung, a camp for relatives of the Workmen's Circle (my grandpop's organization for garment workers) in 1951, there was an outbreak of polio the second day I was there. This was before the polio vaccine, and everyone had to receive a gamma globulin shot. For the remainder of my two-week stay, Camp Hofnung was quarantined. As bad as that was, it took almost a week for my tush to stop hurting from the huge needle used for the injection.

After a lot of negative reasoning on my part, Jane wore me down and finally convinced me that camp would be a great experience for Alexandra. She turned out to be correct. The three of us visited a number of prospective camps and ultimately agreed to an all-girls camp, Lake Bryn Mawr, in Honesdale, Pennsylvania. It was the one camp where we felt our daughter would be safe, that didn't smell from dank sour milk in the dining room, and that had the nicest social and athletic facilities.

For me, as the father of a daughter, the "no boys" aspect of the camp was the key affirmation that this was the best camp for our little girl.

Alexandra had just turned ten years old when she spent her first eight weeks as a camper. She loved it and went there for three more years. All the kids and their parents meet at the King of Prussia Mall to get the campers on the buses that take them to camp each year. Each June for the departure, I always see several moms weeping and their husbands comforting them.

Jane is fine, and I suck it up until Alexandra gets on the bus, and then I break down. It is Jane's turn to comfort me.

Around that time we have a few friends who brag about how happy they are when that camp bus leaves with their kids each summer.

They are beyond happy. They are giddy.

I can never understand how any parent feels that way.

Eventually we drop those friends.

I never failed seeing Josh in a football game or Noah in a basketball game when we live in Florida. After we move back north, Noah is in the drumline of the Wissahickon High School marching band. Although Jane is pregnant for most of that period, she and I go to every one of Noah's band competitions.

Alexandra was a cheerleader at Germantown Academy and co-captain of the squad in her junior and senior years. Jane and I attend all the football games and cheerleading tournaments. Actually Jane attends most football games. There are a few away games at Malvern Prep, Haverford, and Episcopal Academy that occur in rain and snow where I am literally the only spectator in the GA stands. It is actually a blessing for the cheerleaders that I am there at those games, because other than the GA football team and coaches, I am the only person on the GA side of the field who knows the difference between offense and defense.

The last cheer the football team wants to hear from the GA cheerleaders when we have the ball is "Take the T to the A to the K to the E—Take that ball away!"

Victim or Master

It's your choice.

Going through life blaming others or uncontrollable circumstances for your unhappiness is the easy way out. No matter how bad life may suck, it remains comfortable for those who choose to be the perennial victim. "Poor me, I can't get a break" and "It's life doing it to me" are the rally cries of those who consider themselves eternally unfortunate. The alternative is to take total responsibility and ownership for your life. Once you are there, there is no turning back.

It is a double-edged sword when you own it all.

At times your whole board may be lit red in the danger zone, and there is no one else to blame. On the other hand, recognizing that life is like a roller-coaster ride and knowing that you are the master in creating your life allows for a real experience of living and the wonderfulness that goes with it. Taking responsibility is empowering. Own it all, and your life will change.

Adversity can become a real positive if you learn from it and draw strength from the memory of "I got through that". This is really hard to do when the roller coaster is in its deepest dive, but if you can stop and recall the past hardships you've overcome, it will definitely lessen the angst of your problems du jour.

Some of my most profound life lessons have taken place in pain and despair.

Have your life be the most important life you've ever experienced.

Friends

Real friends are people who never forget how terrific you are—even when you do.

Unconditional Love

Truly accepting people for who they are and who they're not.

Communication

Communication is also listening.

One of the best takeaways for me from doing comedy improvisation is that it is the best exercise in listening and thinking on your feet anyone could have.

Think about it; you can go to the gym or work with a trainer to exercise every muscle in your body. Where else can you go to exercise your brain to stop thinking about how you are going to respond before you hear what is actually said?

In comedy improvisation your mind must be totally clear of any preconceived thoughts. When the other person says, "The sky is such a beautiful shade of orange today," your response cannot be "What have you been smoking?" In comedy improv you learn that whatever the other person says becomes the immediate factual state of things. You have to totally listen to the other person to be able to respond to his or her reality. "You know what? You are so right. I don't think I ever saw it before so magnificently orange."

The success of every relationship, whether it's with your business associates, your friends, your spouse or your children, is a function of communication.

Listening and responding to what others are truly saying and feeling is what's critical.

Favorite People

One of my all-time favorite people is my twelfth grade high school English teacher, Mrs. Thelma O'Brien. She was the most sparkling, enthusiastic, vivacious, gray-haired lady I have ever known. She reveled in her love for life. Although she never mentioned it, there was a rumor that her son died when he was a teenager.

Mrs. O'Brien would often say, "People are more fun than anybody." She was truly an inspiration for anyone who knew her.

Craziness

I believe everyone is allowed to have one thing in life for which she/he has an unexplainable and unfounded disgust and loathing that any rational person would describe as utter craziness.

For me that thing is margarine.

The sight, smell, or mere thought of margarine brings waves of nausea to me. It's not that I eat a lot of butter either, but there is something about margarine that makes me gag. I read every food label to make sure that there is no oleo inside, and I question waiters and waitresses if I have any doubt about what's in a dish or how it is prepared. I dislike eating someone else's home-cooked meal because I am not sure what ingredients were used.

For years I repressed how I developed this visceral feeling, until one day I had an epiphany about how my abhorrence of margarine began. When I am a freshman at Central High School, it is the first time I ever purchase lunch at school. After trying numerous daily offerings in the lunchroom, I discover that most of it is inedible until one day I discover PB&J. "Now this is something I can eat," I think.

After that experience I become hooked on peanut butter and jelly sandwiches. In fact, I am a daily PB&J lover for a few months until one day I notice some whitish stuff hanging out the side of my sandwich. "Uh-oh, what is this?" my inquiring mind wants to know. "This viscous substance resembles neither peanut butter nor jelly." That's when I approach the counter and look beyond the display to the preparation table. There, two ladies with nets on their hair are slathering this white stuff on what appears to be hundreds of slices of white bread. This gloppy spread is the mandatory base for whatever will be added to the bread.

It could be peanut butter, it could be jelly, or it could be baloney.

It didn't matter. The substrate of *every* sandwich is white bread and this unidentified substance.

I see the hairnet ladies repetitively diving with their spatulas into this tub, and I strain to read the writing on the label of the huge plastic jar.

There it is. I can read it. It says, "MARGARINE."

Needless to say, this immediately ends my PB&J fervor, and al-though I don't realize it at the time, I will be forever damaged by this discovery.

To be totally honest with you, I am actually getting nauseated just writing this.

Whatever your craziness is, I believe that we are each given one divine special dispensation, requiring no explanation on your part, to loathe the bane of your existence as much as margarine is mine.

Integrity

It's OK that not everyone likes me.

What is important is that I like me and that I remain true to myself.

If you do what you say you will do and do it when you say you will do it, that weighty bag of intentions and promises you carry around on your back will disappear.

You will be happier and your back will stop hurting.

(XI)
FREE PRIZE INSIDE

CHAPTER 58

Hiccups

JUST IN CASE my writings have had no lasting value for you, I present to you this final gift. Once you have utilized it, you will affirm that it is more than worth the price of admission.

When I was in my twenties, I read a physician's comment about hiccups in the *Journal of the American Medical Association*. This doctor's avocation was translating Sanskrit tablets, and while doing so, he came across a cure for hiccups. His inquiry to JAMA was to see if anyone could provide some medical justification for this almost one hundred percent cure that he had deciphered. No one was able to respond with a scientific rationale. In spite of the lack of any medical explanation, I have tried it numerous times on anyone in my line of sight who had hiccups, and it has absolutely worked every time.

This has never failed with Josh, Noah, or me.

It even works on girls. Jane and Alexandra are also testament to this no-fail hiccup remedy.

It goes like this:

Place a silver or stainless steel knife in a tall glass of cold water. Hold the part of the knife protruding from the glass against your temple and keep the rest of the knife immersed in the glass while you drink the water. Drink the water and, *voila*, no more hiccups!

Remember this, and try it the next time you or someone next to you has hiccups.

You will be amazed, and you may even take a moment to reflect about the guy who gave you this cure,

"Not bad for a Philly boy; not bad for a pharmacist."

P. 9

9/11/06   Penn

Alexandre

P 199

Humane - Zilch

Life's Barometer   -plants

Callaghach

drums / pharmacist

The Bulletin (o)

Lois
June
Jane

CPSIA information can be obtained
at www.ICGtesting.com
Printed in the USA
BVHW040457220620
581984BV00003B/85

9 781478 714934